Chemistry

for Cambridge IGCSE™

MATHS SKILLS WORKBOOK

Helen Harden

CAMBRIDGE
UNIVERSITY PRESS

University Printing House, Cambridge CB2 8BS, United Kingdom

One Liberty Plaza, 20th Floor, New York, NY 10006, USA

477 Williamstown Road, Port Melbourne, VIC 3207, Australia

314–321, 3rd Floor, Plot 3, Splendor Forum, Jasola District Centre, New Delhi – 110025, India

103 Penang Road, 05–06/07, Visioncrest Commercial, Singapore 238467

Cambridge University Press is part of the University of Cambridge.

It furthers the University's mission by disseminating knowledge in the pursuit of education,
learning and research at the highest international levels of excellence.

www.cambridge.org
Information on this title: www.cambridge.org/9781108948364

First edition 2018
Second edition 2022

20 19 18 17 16 15 14 13 12 11 10 9 8 7 6 5 4 3 2 1

Printed in Italy by L.E.G.O. S.p.A.

A catalogue record for this publication is available from the British Library

ISBN 978-1-108-94836-4 Maths Skills Workbook Paperback

Additional resources for this publication at www.cambridge.org/9781108948364

Illustrations by Tech-Set

DEDICATED TEACHER AWARDS

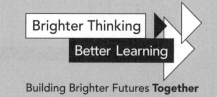

> Contents

How to use this series   vi

How to use this book   viii

Introduction   ix

Maths skills grid   x

Chapter	Area of focus	Skills to develop	Page
1 Representing values	Maths focus 1: Using units	Maths skill 1: Choosing the correct unit	4
		Maths skill 2: Writing the unit symbol	6
		Maths skill 3: Writing symbols for derived units	8
	Maths focus 2: Understanding very large and very small numbers	Maths skill 1: Understanding place value	12
		Maths skill 2: Understanding powers of ten	13
		Maths skill 3: Understanding unit prefixes	16
	Maths focus 3: Writing numbers in a required form	Maths skill 1: Writing numbers in standard form	19
		Maths skill 2: Writing numbers to the required number of significant figures	23
2 Working with data	Maths focus 1: Collecting data	Maths skill 1: Reading scales	30
		Maths skill 2: Recording to the correct number of decimal places	33
	Maths focus 2: Understanding types of data	Maths skill 1: Identifying independent and dependent variables	38
		Maths skill 2: Distinguishing categorical, continuous and discrete data	39
	Maths focus 3: Recording and processing data	Maths skill 1: Drawing tables	42
		Maths skill 2: Drawing tables to help process data	45
		Maths skill 3: Recording processed data to the correct number of significant figures	48
3 Drawing charts and graphs	Maths focus 1: Drawing bar charts	Maths skill 1: Choosing a suitable scale for the vertical axis (y-axis)	56
		Maths skill 2: Drawing the bars	58
	Maths focus 2: Drawing pie charts	Maths skill 1: Converting percentages to angles	65
		Maths skill 2: Drawing the sectors	66
	Maths focus 3: Drawing line graphs	Maths skill 1: Choosing which variable goes on which axis	74
		Maths skill 2: Drawing the axes	75
		Maths skill 3: Plotting the data points	79
		Maths skill 4: Using a ruler to draw a best-fit line	80
		Maths skill 5: Drawing a best-fit curve freehand	83

Contents

Chapter	Area of focus	Skills to develop	Page
4 Interpreting data	Maths focus 1: Interpreting charts	Maths skill 1: Interpreting the heights of bars on a bar chart	94
		Maths skill 2: Comparing the sizes of sectors on a pie chart	97
	Maths focus 2: Reading values from a line graph	Maths skill 1: Interpolating line graphs	101
		Maths skill 2: Extrapolating line graphs	104
		Maths skill 3: Finding the intercept	106
	Maths focus 3: Interpreting the shape of line graphs	Maths skill 1: Recognising the shape of the graph	113
		Maths skill 2: Interpreting the changing gradient of a curve	115
		Maths skill 3: Calculating the gradient of a straight-line graph	118
		Maths skill 4: Calculating the gradient by drawing a tangent to the curve	122
5 Doing calculations	Maths focus 1: Using basic mathematical operations in calculations	Maths skills 1: Working out the correct calculation for relative formula mass	133
		Maths skill 2: Using mathematical operations in the correct order to calculate relative formula mass	135
		Maths skill 3: Calculating the number of particles using powers of ten	136
		Maths skill 4: Using positive and negative values to interpret the overall enthalpy change of a chemical reaction	137
	Maths focus 2: Calculating and using percentages	Maths skill 1: Calculating percentage composition by mass	141
		Maths skill 2: Calculating percentage yield	143
		Maths skill 3: Calculating percentage purity	145
		Maths skill 4: Using percentages to calculate relative atomic mass	146
	Maths focus 3: Using mathematical formulae in calculations	Maths skill 1: Substituting values into a mathematical formula	149
		Maths skill 2: Rearranging a mathematical formula	152
		Maths skill 3: Using titration results to calculate the concentration of a solution	155
	Maths focus 4: Calculating using proportional relationships	Maths skill 1: Recognising directly and indirectly proportional relationships	160
	Maths focus 5: Calculating using ratios	Maths skill 1: Using ratio to work out reacting masses	165
		Maths skill 2: Using ratio and moles to work out reacting masses	168
6 Working with shape	Maths focus 1: Comparing surface area and volume	Maths skill 1: Calculating surface area	177
		Maths skill 2: Comparing the surface area to volume ratio	181

Applying more than one skill 188

Glossary 206

Appendix: The Periodic Table 209

Acknowledgements 210

> How to use this series

We offer a comprehensive, flexible array of resources for the Cambridge IGCSE™ Chemistry syllabus. We provide targeted support and practice for the specific challenges we've heard that students face: learning science with English as a second language; learners who find the mathematical content within science difficult; and developing practical skills.

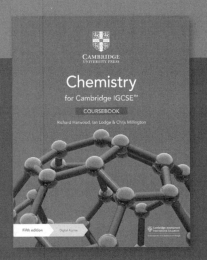

The coursebook provides coverage of the full Cambridge IGCSE Chemistry syllabus. Each chapter explains facts and concepts, and uses relevant real-world examples of scientific principles to bring the subject to life. Together with a focus on practical work and plenty of active learning opportunities, the coursebook prepares learners for all aspects of their scientific study. At the end of each chapter, examination-style questions offer practice opportunities for learners to apply their learning.

The digital teacher's resource contains detailed guidance for all topics of the syllabus, including common misconceptions identifying areas where learners might need extra support, as well as an engaging bank of lesson ideas for each syllabus topic. Differentiation is emphasised with advice for identification of different learner needs and suggestions of appropriate interventions to support and stretch learners. The teacher's resource also contains support for preparing and carrying out all the investigations in the practical workbook, including a set of sample results for when practicals aren't possible.

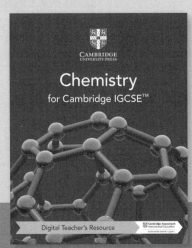

The teacher's resource also contains scaffolded worksheets and unit tests for each chapter. Answers for all components are accessible to teachers for free on the Cambridge GO platform.

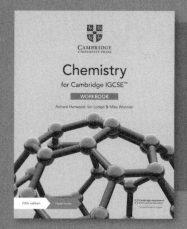

The skills-focused workbook has been carefully constructed to help learners develop the skills that they need as they progress through their Cambridge IGCSE Chemistry course, providing further practice of all the topics in the coursebook. A three-tier, scaffolded approach to skills development enables students to gradually progress through 'focus', 'practice' and 'challenge' exercises, ensuring that every learner is supported. The workbook enables independent learning and is ideal for use in class or as homework.

The practical workbook provides learners with additional opportunities for hands-on practical work, giving them full guidance and support that will help them to develop their investigative skills. These skills include planning investigations, selecting and handling apparatus, creating hypotheses, recording and displaying results, and analysing and evaluating data.

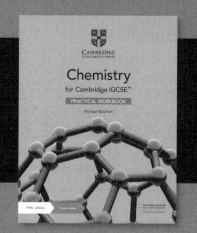

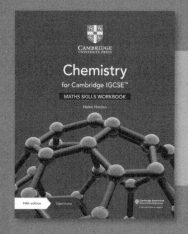

Mathematics is an integral part of scientific study, and one that learners often find a barrier to progression in science. The Cambridge IGCSE Chemistry write-in maths skills workbook has been written in collaboration with the Association for Science Education, with each chapter focusing on several maths skills that students need to succeed in their Chemistry course.

Our research shows that English language skills are the single biggest barrier to students accessing international science. This write-in English language skills workbook contains exercises set within the context of Cambridge IGCSE Chemistry topics to consolidate understanding and embed practice in aspects of language central to the subject. Activities range from practising using the passive form of the verbs in the context of electrolysis to the naming of chemical substances using common prefixes.

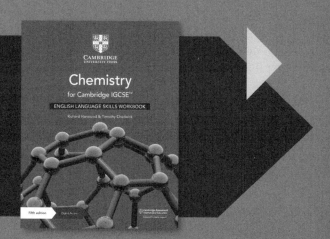

> How to use this book

Throughout this book, you will notice lots of different features that will help your learning.

OVERVIEW

This sets the scene for each chapter, and explains why the maths skills in that chapter are important for you to understand.

WORKED EXAMPLES

These show a maths concept in action, giving you a step-by-step guide to answering a question related to that concept.

LOOK OUT

The information in these boxes will help you complete the questions, and give you support in areas that you might find difficult.

Questions

Questions give you a chance to practise the skills in each Maths focus. You can find the answers to these questions in the Teacher's Resource.

EXAM-STYLE QUESTIONS

Questions at the end of each chapter provide more demanding exam-style questions. Answers to these questions can be found in the Teacher's Resource.

Applying more than one skill

At the end of this Workbook you will find a section of exam-style questions covering any of the topics covered in the chapters. This will give you a chance to think about how to apply your maths skills to different contexts.

Throughout the book, you will see important words in **bold** font. You will find definitions for these words in the Key Words boxes and in the Glossary at the back of the book. Command words that appear in the syllabus and might be used in exams are also highlighted in the exam-style questions. In the margin, you will find the Cambridge International definition.

> Supplement content

Where content is intended for students who are studying the Supplement content of the syllabus as well as the Core, this is indicated with the arrow and bar, as you can see on the left here.

〉 Introduction

This workbook has been written to help you to improve your skills in the mathematical processes that you need in your Cambridge IGCSE™ Chemistry course and fully covers the mathematical syllabus content. The exercises will guide you and give you practice in:

- representing values

- working with data

- drawing charts and graphs

- interpreting data

- doing calculations

- working with shape.

Each chapter focuses on several maths skills that you need to master to be successful in your Chemistry course and explains why you need these skills. Then, for each skill, there is a step-by-step worked example of a question that involves the skill. This is followed by questions for you to try. These are not like exam questions. They are designed to develop your skills and understanding. They get increasingly challenging. Advice is given in the Look Out boxes to help guide you. Spaces, lines or graph grids are provided for your answers.

It is best to work through Chapters 1 and 2 early in your course, as they will help to ensure that you have a secure understanding of number and units, as well as confidence in reading scales when making measurements. Chapter 3 shows you the skills you need to draw a variety of different types of chart and graph. These chapters will support you with many practical activities that you may carry out.

Chapter 4 covers the skills needed to read information from charts and graphs, as well as the specific graph skills that you will need when studying rates of reaction. Chapter 6 shows you the mathematics of the ratio of surface area to volume, which will help to explain why changing surface area affects the rate of reaction.

A few of the maths concepts and skills are only needed if you are following the Extended syllabus (Core plus Supplement). Most of these are in Chapter 5, which covers the key calculations needed in chemistry, including the use of moles (Supplement only).

There are exam-style questions at the end of each chapter for you to try, using the skills practised within the chapter. At the end of the book, there are additional questions that may require any of the maths skills from all of the chapters.

Note for teachers:

Additional teaching ideas for this Maths Skills Workbook are available on Cambridge GO, downloadable with this workbook and the Cambridge IGCSE Chemistry Teacher's Resource. This includes engaging activities to use in lessons, with guidance on differentiation and assessment.

Answers to all questions in this Maths Skills Workbook are also accessible to teachers at www.cambridge.org/go

> Maths skills grid

The mathematical requirements focus on skills that you will need in your Cambridge IGCSE Chemistry course. Each of the mathematical requirements have been broken down for you with a reference to the chapters in this book that cover it. This will enable you to identify where you have practised each skill and also allow you to revise each one before your exams.

The information in this section is taken from the Cambridge International syllabus (0620/0971) for examination from 2023. You should always refer to the appropriate syllabus document for the year of your examination to confirm the details and for more information. The syllabus document is available on the Cambridge International website www.cambridgeinternational.org.

	Chapter 1	Chapter 2	Chapter 3	Chapter 4	Chapter 5	Chapter 6
Number						
Add, subtract, multiply and divide	▓	▓				
Use decimals, fractions, percentages, ratios and reciprocals	▓	▓				
Use standard form	▓					
Understand that only the final answer in a calculation is rounded	▓					
Use decimal places and significant figures appropriately	▓					
Algebra						
Use positive whole number indices in algebraic expressions					▓	
Substitute values of quantities into equations, using consistent units						
Solve simple algebraic equations for any one term when the other terms are known					▓	
Recognise and use direct and inverse proportion					▓	
Geometry and measurements						
Understand the meaning of angle, curve, radius, diameter, circumference, square, rectangle and diagonal			▓			▓

	Chapter 1	Chapter 2	Chapter 3	Chapter 4	Chapter 5	Chapter 6
Select and use the most appropriate units for recording data and the results of calculations	▪					
Convert between units, including cm^3 and dm^3; mg, g and kg; J and kJ; Pa and kPa	▪					
Graphs, charts and statistics						
Draw graphs and charts from data		▪	▪			
Interpret graphs and charts, including interpolation and extrapolation of data				▪		
Determine the gradient (slope) of a line of a graph, including by drawing a tangent to a curve				▪		
Determine the intercept of the line on a graph, extending the line graphically (extrapolating) where appropriate				▪		
Select suitable scales and axes for graphs			▪			
Recognise direct proportionality from a graph			▪			
Calculate and use the mean (average) for a set of data		▪				

> Representing values

WHY DO YOU NEED TO REPRESENT VALUES IN CHEMISTRY?

- You need to be able to communicate any measurements that you make.

- You must make sure that another person is able to understand your measurements, so how you represent (write down) the measurements is important. As well as the numerical value, you must also include the correct unit.

- You need to be able to understand numbers that are much larger or much smaller than numbers you usually work with. Writing these numbers in different ways will make measurements easier to understand and compare.

Maths focus 1: Using units

KEY WORDS

index: a small raised number that indicates the power, for example, the index 4 here shows that the 2 is raised to the power 4, which means four 2s multiplied together: $2^4 = 2 \times 2 \times 2 \times 2$

scale: a set of marks with equal intervals, for example, on a graph axis or a measuring cylinder, or, on a scale diagram, the ratio of a length in the diagram to the actual size

unit: a standard used in measuring a variable, for example, the metre or the volt

Units of measurements used in chemistry are based upon the international system of units (SI).

Table 1.1 shows some SI base units that are commonly used in chemistry.

Quantity	Unit	SI abbreviation
length	metre	m
mass	kilogram	kg
time	second	s
amount of substance	mole	mol

Table 1.1: SI base units for common quantities.

The SI base unit for temperature is the kelvin (K), but the Celsius **scale** (°C) is more useful for many laboratory measurements in chemistry. Most thermometers use the Celsius scale. On the Celsius scale, the freezing point of water is 0 °C and the boiling point of water (at 1 atmosphere pressure) is 100 °C.

What maths skills do you need to be able to use units?

LOOK OUT

Remember that a temperature can have a negative value on the Celsius scale, such as −4 °C.

1	Choosing the correct unit	• Identify the type of quantity that the apparatus measures.
		• Select an appropriate unit for the quantity being measured.
2	Writing the unit symbol	• Recall or look up the unit symbol.
		• Check if the unit requires **index** notation, for example, cm^2 or cm^3.
3	Writing symbols for derived units	• Work out how the quantity is calculated.
		• Write the derived unit, which is based on the units in the calculation.

Maths skills practice

How can units help you to communicate values that you measure during chemical reactions?

KEY WORDS

power of ten: a number such as 10^3 or 10^{-3}

ratio: a comparison of two numbers or of two measurements with the same unit; the ratio of A to B can be written $A:B$ or expressed as a fraction $\frac{A}{B}$

unit prefix: a prefix (term added to the front of a word) added to a unit name to indicate a power of ten of that unit, e.g. 1 millimetre = 10^{-3} metre

LOOK OUT

The kilogram (kg) is the only base SI unit whose name and symbol, for historical reasons, use a prefix.

When you do experimental (practical) work in chemistry, always use the appropriate units when you record any measurements.

It is meaningless to give the volume of gas produced during a chemical reaction simply as '16'. Using units clearly specifies (describes) the volume measured. A volume of $16 cm^3$ is completely different from a volume of 16 litres.

A mass of 3 g is one thousand times smaller than 3 kg, so it is essential to use the correct **unit prefix** as well as the correct unit. The unit prefix tells you the **power of ten** by which to multiply the measurement.

See Maths skills 2 and 3 in Maths focus 2 for more information about powers of ten and unit prefixes.

Most values used in chemistry require units because they are measures of particular quantities, such as:

- length
- mass
- temperature
- time
- volume
- amount of a substance.

LOOK OUT

Not all values require units. For example, relative atomic mass is a simple **ratio** (a comparison of two numbers) and therefore does not need units.

Maths skill 1: Choosing the correct unit

It is important that you know the names of the units that are often used for measurements in chemistry.

WORKED EXAMPLE 1.1

Choose the correct unit of measurement associated with the small beaker shown in Figure 1.1.

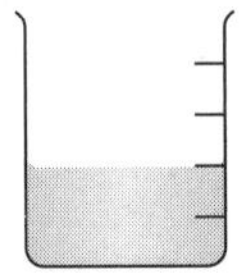

Figure 1.1: A beaker.

A centimetres
B litres
C square centimetres
D cubic centimetres

Step 1: Identify the type of quantity that the apparatus measures.

A beaker measures volume.

Step 2: Select an appropriate unit for the quantity being measured.

Key questions to ask yourself:

- What units are used to measure this type of quantity?

  Volume may be measured in a variety of units, including litres (l) or cubic centimetres (cm^3).

- Which units are appropriate for the scale on the measuring apparatus?

  A small beaker will not measure litres (l). The scale is likely to be in cubic centimetres (cm^3).

So, the correct answer is D (cubic centimetres).

LOOK OUT

In chemistry you usually use dm^3.
1 dm^3 = 1 litre

LOOK OUT

You may see measuring equipment that is marked in millilitres (mL).
1mL = 1cm^3

LOOK OUT

Always stop and think, 'Are the units appropriate for the measuring apparatus that is being used?'

Questions

1   Draw lines to connect each item of measuring apparatus with the appropriate unit of measurement.

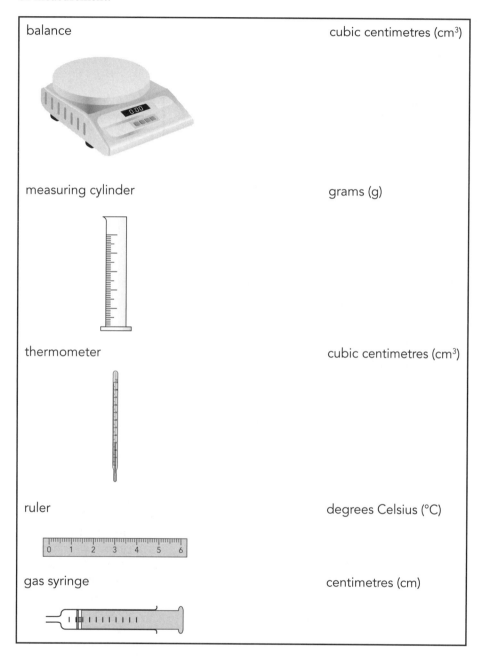

balance   cubic centimetres (cm³)

measuring cylinder   grams (g)

thermometer   cubic centimetres (cm³)

ruler   degrees Celsius (°C)

gas syringe   centimetres (cm)

2   Work in pairs. Choose a unit of measurement. Ask your partner to name a piece of chemistry apparatus that can be used to measure the unit you have chosen.

Check your partner's answer. Has your partner chosen apparatus that is the correct size for measuring the unit?

Now swap roles and start again, so that your partner names a unit and you name the piece of apparatus.

LOOK OUT

A small measuring cylinder does measure **volume**, but it is unlikely to measure in litres.

Maths skill 2: Writing the unit symbol

When you write down measurements from an experiment, you do not need to write the name of the units in full. Each unit has a symbol. This is an abbreviation (short version) that uses one, two or three letters (Table 1.2).

Quantity	Unit	Symbol
length	metre	m
mass	kilogram	kg
time	second	s
temperature	degrees Celsius	°C
amount of substance	mole	mol

Table 1.2: Symbols for some commonly used base units.

Most base unit symbols start with a lower-case letter and not a capital letter (e.g. metres are abbreviated as 'm' not 'M'). Some other unit symbols start with a capital letter.

Other units are created by placing a prefix in front of the SI unit. For example, centimetres (cm) are used for measuring shorter distances than metres (m).

1 cm is $\frac{1}{100}$ m or 0.01 m.

See Maths skills 3 in Maths focus 2 for more information about unit prefixes.

Always remember to include the correct index or **power** when necessary. The index is the small number to the right and above the base number that tells you the power (how many times you need to multiply the base number by itself). Three squared (3×3) is written as 3^2. The index '2' shows you that the power is 2, so $3 \times 3 = 9$.

LOOK OUT

Remember to think about whether the unit needs a capital letter or not. A unit symbol starts with a capital letter if it is named after a person. For example, the Celsius temperature scale is named after the Swedish astronomer Anders Celsius.

It is incorrect to write a volume of liquid as 10 cm because centimetres are a unit of length.

- **Area** is always measured in *square* units (such as m² or cm²). You calculate the area of a rectangle by multiplying length × width, for example, m × m or cm × cm (think about counting squares on a grid to find areas).

- **Volume** is always measured in *cubic* units (such as m³ or cm³). You calculate the volume of a cuboid by multiplying length × width × height, for example, m × m × m or cm × cm × cm (think about counting cubes in a cuboid made from unit cubes as shown in Figure 1.2).

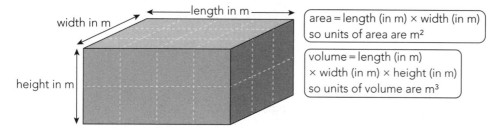

area = length (in m) × width (in m)
so units of area are m²

volume = length (in m)
× width (in m) × height (in m)
so units of volume are m³

Figure 1.2: Comparing the area of a face and the volume of a cuboid.

WORKED EXAMPLE 1.2

The length and the width of a piece of paper have been measured in centimetres. Write down the correct unit for the area of the paper.

Step 1: Recall or look up the unit symbol.

The unit symbol for the measurements is cm (centimetres).

Step 2: Check if the unit requires index notation.

Area is found by multiplying length by width (cm × cm), so area must be measured in *square* units. This is shown by using an index of '2'.

The unit is square centimetres (cm²).

Questions

3 **a** Write down the correct unit symbol for each measurement.

  i Mass of copper sulfate, measured on a digital balance that measures in grams. ....

  ii Temperature of water, measured using a thermometer marked in degrees Celsius. ....

  iii Time taken for a reaction to occur, measured using a stopwatch that displays seconds. ....

  iv Length of magnesium ribbon, measured using a ruler marked in centimetres. ....

    v   Area of the floor in a laboratory, where the length and
the width are measured in metres.   ....

    vi   Volume of liquid in a measuring cylinder that is marked
in cubic centimetres.   ....

b   Check your partner's answers from part **a**. Complete the checklist in your
partner's workbook.

	Was index notation required?	Was index notation used?
i	☐	☐
ii	☐	☐
iii	☐	☐
iv	☐	☐
v	☐	☐
vi	☐	☐

4   Work in pairs. Discuss with your partner why index notation is important for
writing units. You should include the following words in your explanation.
You may use each word more than once.

        length(s)   **area**   **volume**   **index**   **units**

Write down your explanation.

....

....

....

....

....

....

Maths skill 3: Writing symbols for derived units

The units for some quantities are based on a calculation using other units. The units
obtained are called **derived units**. For example, when a chemical reaction produces
a gas, you can calculate the **rate** of reaction (how fast the reaction takes place) by
dividing the volume of gas produced by the time taken to collect this volume of gas.
If the volume is measured in cubic centimetres (cm^3) and the time is measured in
seconds (s), the derived unit of rate of reaction is cubic centimetres per second (cm^3/s).

> **LOOK OUT**
>
> The symbol '/'
> (known as a solidus)
> is also used as a
> separator between a
> **variable** name and
> its unit, in tables
> and on graphs.
> Here, you read the
> '/' sign as 'in', so
> 'Temperature / °C'
> means 'temperature
> in degrees Celsius'.

WORKED EXAMPLE 1.3

The density of a substance is the mass of the substance that occupies a particular volume. You can calculate the density of an aluminium cube by dividing the mass of the cube (in grams) by the volume of the cube (in cubic centimetres).

Write down the correct derived unit for density.

Step 1: Work out how the quantity is calculated.

The calculation for density is:

$$density = \frac{mass}{volume}$$

Step 2: Write the derived unit, which is based on the units in the calculation.

The derived unit is grams per cubic centimetre (g/cm^3).

Questions

5 Write down the correct derived unit for each calculated quantity:

   a The rate of a chemical reaction, calculated by dividing the mass of product made (in grams) by the time taken for the reaction (in seconds).   ....

   b The density of a large metal statue, calculated by dividing the mass of the statue (in kilograms) by its volume (in cubic metres).   ....

6 Work in pairs. The units of a rate of reaction are cm^3/s. Discuss with your partner what this tells you about how the product of this chemical reaction is measured and write down your answer.

   ....

   ....

Maths focus 2: Understanding very large and very small numbers

KEY WORDS

decimal: a number expressed using a system of counting based on the number 10 (e.g. three fifths expressed as a decimal is 0.6); the number consists of a whole number and a fractional part separated by a decimal point

diameter: a straight line connecting two points on a circle (or sphere) that passes through the centre

digit: any of the numerals from 0 to 9 used to make a number

place value: the value of a digit depending on its position within a number, for example, in 476, there are 4 hundreds, 7 tens and 6 units

reciprocal: 1 divided by a value; for example, the reciprocal of A is $\frac{1}{A}$

In chemistry, you need to understand very large numbers.

- 12 g of carbon contains about 602 000 000 000 000 000 000 000 atoms.

You also need to understand very small numbers.

- A single carbon atom has a **diameter** of about 0.000 000 000 17 m. It is very important to use the correct number of zeros. The value of the number depends upon the **place value** of the **digits**. If you use the wrong number of zeros, the value will change.

However, writing out this many zeros takes a lot of time, so very large and very small numbers are often written using powers of ten instead of many zeros.
Also, such numbers can easily be misread. This can result in the number of zeros being miscounted, leading to errors.

- The number of atoms in 12 g of carbon can also be written as 6.02×10^{23}.

- The diameter of a carbon atom can also be written as 1.7×10^{-10} m.

6.02×10^{23} is an important number in chemistry and is also known as the Avogadro constant.

Sometimes the units are changed for very large and very small numbers by adding a prefix to the unit, such as kilo- (k) or nano- (n). These prefixes replace the power of ten.

So, $3 \text{ kg} = 3 \times 10^3 \text{ g}$ or 3000 g

See Maths skill 3 for more information about unit prefixes used in chemistry.

What maths skills do you need to be able to understand very large and very small numbers?

1	Understanding place value	• Compare the digits with the highest place value.
		• Compare the digits with the next highest place values.
2	Understanding powers of ten	• Write out the multiplication.
		• Calculate the number as it would be written in full.
3	Understanding unit prefixes	• Write the measurement using a power of ten.
		• Calculate the number as it would be written in full.

Maths skills practice

How does understanding very large and very small numbers help to improve your understanding of the size and number of different particles?

Some numbers used in chemistry are so large, or so small, that they are difficult to imagine. Writing these numbers in a clearer way, such as using powers of ten or prefixes, helps you understand how the size of different particles compare.

Particulate air pollution is made of very small particles of pollutants (substances present in the atmosphere, such as dust and carbon produced by industry, vehicles and burning fossil fuels). These particles have different sizes and are given a PM (particulate matter) number based on their diameter.

A particle of $PM_{2.5}$ air pollution has a diameter of about 2.5×10^{-6} m or $2.5\,\mu m$, whereas a particle of PM_{10} air pollution is about 10×10^{-6} m or $10\,\mu m$ in diameter. If you understand powers of ten and unit prefixes, you can instantly see that these particles are much larger than a typical atom, which is about 1×10^{-10} m in diameter.

Before you can compare sizes like this, it is important that you have a good understanding of place value in numbers that are written out in full.

Maths skill 1: Understanding place value

The place value of a digit is based on the digit's position in a number. The left-most digit in a number has the highest place value. For example, the number in Table 1.3 (reading from left to right) is:

three hundred and twenty-three billion, four hundred and fifty-six million, three hundred and forty-five thousand, six hundred and forty-seven

Hundreds of billions	Tens of billions	Billions	Hundreds of millions	Tens of millions	Millions	Hundreds of thousands	Tens of thousands	Thousands	Hundreds	Tens	Units
10^{11}	10^{10}	10^{9}	10^{8}	10^{7}	10^{6}	10^{5}	10^{4}	10^{3}	10^{2}	10^{1}	10^{0}
3	2	3	4	5	6	3	4	5	6	4	7

Table 1.3: Place values for large numbers.

The **decimal** fraction in Table 1.4 is one billionth.

Units		Tenths	Hundredths	Thousandths	Ten-thousandths	Hundred-thousandths	Millionths	Ten-millionths	Hundred-millionths	Billionths
0	.	0	0	0	0	0	0	0	0	1

Table 1.4: Place values for small numbers.

WORKED EXAMPLE 1.4

Find the largest number in the following list:

A   7 242 519   B   8 143 921   C   8 349 321   D   924 107

Step 1: Compare the digits with the highest place value.

A, B and C all have millions as the highest place value.
B and C both have digits showing 8 million, so are larger than A, which has 7 million.

Step 2: Compare the digits with the next highest place values.

The next highest place value is hundreds of thousands.
B has 1 hundred thousand, but C has 3 hundred thousand.
So, the largest number is C.

Questions

LOOK OUT

Read the number from left to right. The place value of the first non-zero number helps you decide how big the number is.

7   Draw a circle around the *largest* number in each list.

a	674 591	92 342	141 294	692 381
b	1 943 986	1 949 789	1 942 987	1 944 098
c	0.09	0.12	0.17	0.06
d	0.09	0.015	0.026	0.07
e	0.000 007 2	0.000 008 5	0.000 000 1	0.000 000 165

8   Draw a circle around the *smallest* number in each list.

a	1 232 452	123 532	723 453	115 362
b	0.123 451	0.345 984	0.135 034	0.124 093
c	0.000 002 234	0.000 002	0.000 002 4	0.000 002 34
d	234.56	234.25	232.12	232.013 4
e	104 985.99	110 374.12	104 895.99	104 895.82

9   Table 1.5 shows the diameter of different atoms in metres.

Atom	Diameter / m
krypton	0.000 000 000 404
helium	0.000 000 000 280
neon	0.000 000 000 308

Table 1.5: Diameter of different atoms.

a   List the atoms in order of diameter from the smallest to the largest.

....

b   Work in pairs. Explain to your partner how you worked out the order of diameter.

Maths skill 2: Understanding powers of ten

Powers of ten are the result of multiplying 10 by itself (Table 1.6).

A negative power of any number is the **reciprocal** of the corresponding positive power.

This means, for example, that $10^{-1} = \frac{1}{10}$ (the reciprocal of 10).

$10^1 = 10$	$10^{-1} = \dfrac{1}{10} = 0.1$
$10^2 = 10 \times 10 = 100$	$10^{-2} = \dfrac{1}{10 \times 10} = \dfrac{1}{100} = 0.01$
$10^5 = 10 \times 10 \times 10 \times 10 \times 10 = 100\,000$	$10^{-5} = \dfrac{1}{10 \times 10 \times 10 \times 10 \times 10} = \dfrac{1}{100\,000}$ $= 1 \div 10 \div 10 \div 10 \div 10 \div 10$

Table 1.6: Powers of ten.

Very large and very small numbers are often recorded as multiples of powers of ten. This makes it easier to write these numbers because you do not have to write lots of zeros.

For example: $4 \times 10^3 = 4 \times 10 \times 10 \times 10 = 4000$

So, multiplying by 10^3 means that you need to multiply by 10 three times (Table 1.7).

4×10^1	4×10	40
4×10^2	$4 \times 10 \times 10$	400
4×10^3	$4 \times 10 \times 10 \times 10$	4000
4×10^4	$4 \times 10 \times 10 \times 10 \times 10$	40\,000
4×10^5	$4 \times 10 \times 10 \times 10 \times 10 \times 10$	400\,000
4×10^6	$4 \times 10 \times 10 \times 10 \times 10 \times 10 \times 10$	4\,000\,000

Table 1.7: Multiplying by powers of ten.

Multiplying a number by a negative power of ten tells you how many times to divide the number by 10.

For example: $4 \times 10^{-3} = 4 \times \dfrac{1}{10 \times 10 \times 10} = 4 \div 10 \div 10 \div 10$

LOOK OUT

Dividing by ten three times is the same as multiplying by 0.001.

WORKED EXAMPLE 1.5

Positive powers of ten

Write 5×10^5 in full.

Step 1: Write out the multiplication.

$$5 \times 10^5 = 5 \times 10 \times 10 \times 10 \times 10 \times 10$$

Step 2: Calculate the number as it would be written in full.

$$= 5 \times 100\,000 = 500\,000$$

> ### WORKED EXAMPLE 1.6
>
> **Negative powers of ten**
>
> Write 3×10^{-4} as a decimal.
>
> **Step 1:** Write out the multiplication.
>
> $$3 \times 10^{-4} = 3 \times \frac{1}{10 \times 10 \times 10 \times 10} = 3 \times 0.0001$$
>
> $$= 3 \div 10 \div 10 \div 10 \div 10$$
>
> **Step 2:** Calculate the number as it would be written in full.
>
> $$= 0.0003$$

Questions

10 These numbers are expressed as multiples of powers of ten. Write the numbers in full.

    a 3×10^3 ....

    b 45×10^6 ....

    c 4×10^1 ....

    d 123×10^{10} ....

11 Write each of these negative powers of ten as a decimal.

    a 2×10^{-2} ....

    b 34×10^{-6} ....

    c 9×10^{-9} ....

    d 43×10^{-5} ....

12 Table 1.8 shows the measurements of different objects in metres. The measurements are written using powers of ten. Complete the table by writing the measurements in full.

Object measurement	Measurement / m	Measurement / m (in full)
length of a water molecule	2.7×10^{-10}	0.000 000 000 27
diameter of a smoke particle	2×10^{-6}	
length of edges of a crystal of table salt	100×10^{-6}	

Table 1.8: Measurements of different objects.

Maths skill 3: Understanding unit prefixes

Rather than writing a number either in full or using powers of ten, you can often just change the unit by using a prefix. The unit prefix tells you the power of ten by which to multiply the measurement to find the full number.

Table 1.9 shows some unit prefixes used in chemistry.

Unit prefix	Unit prefix symbol	Multiplying factor	Example unit names	Example unit symbols
kilo-	k	10^3	kilogram	kg
			kilojoule	kJ
			kilopascal	kPa
deci-	d	10^{-1}	cubic decimetre	dm^3
centi-	c	10^{-2}	cubic centimetre	cm^3
milli-	m	10^{-3}	milligram	mg
			millimetre	mm
micro-	μ	10^{-6}	microgram	μg
			micrometre	μm
nano-	n	10^{-9}	nanometre	nm

Table 1.9: Unit prefixes used in chemistry. Note that the prefixes micro- and nano- are beyond the scope of the syllabus and are not required knowledge.

> **LOOK OUT**
>
> In chemistry, dm^3 are used instead of litres. Think about why 1 litre = 1 dm^3.
>
> 1 dm = 0.1 m or 10 cm
>
> so 1 dm^3 = 10 cm × 10 cm × 10 cm
> = 1000 cm^3
> = 1 litre

WORKED EXAMPLE 1.7

Write 8 mg without using the unit prefix.

Step 1: Write the measurement using a power of ten.

$$8\,mg = 8 \times 10^{-3}\,g$$

Step 2: Calculate the number as it would be written in full.

$$8 \times 10^{-3} = 8 \times \frac{1}{10 \times 10 \times 10}$$

$$= 8 \div 10 \div 10 \div 10 \text{ or } 8 \times 0.001$$

$$= 0.008$$

$$\text{So, } 8\,mg = 8 \times 10^{-3}\,g = 0.008\,g$$

Questions

13 Write each measurement without the unit prefix.

    a   **i**   3 mg ....   **ii**   4 µg ....

          iii 3 kg ....

    b   **i**   4 mm ....   **ii**   2 cm ....

          iii 7 nm ....

    c   **i**   4 cm ....   **ii**   2 dm ....

    d   **i**   5 kJ ....   **ii**   9 kPa ....

14 Write each measurement without the unit prefix.

    a   **i**   42 mg ....   **ii**   402 µg ....

          iii 345 kg ....

    b   **i**   74 nm ....   **ii**   7.4 nm ....

          iii 704 nm ....

    c   **i**   500 kJ ....   **ii**   10 kPa ....

          iii 134 kJ ....

15 Work in groups of three or four. In your group, discuss which unit prefix (k, m, µ, c) should be used for each measurement. Write down your answers individually. Only use each unit prefix once.

    a   **i**   The diameter of a gold coin is 3 .... m.

          ii   The thickness of a gold ring is 3 .... m.

          iii   The mass of a gold bar is 12.4 .... g.

          iv   The thickness of gold leaf (sheet) is 0.1 .... m.

    b   Try to explain how you worked out the appropriate unit prefix for each measurement. How did you compare the measurements of the different objects? Did you picture each object in your mind or use another method? How successful was your way of thinking?

16 a i Write 1000 g using the unit prefix k (kilo). ....

ii Describe to your partner what maths calculation you could use to change from g to kg.

b Write each measurement with the unit prefix k.

i 2000 g ....   **ii** 5000 J ....

iii 3000 Pa ....   **iv** 500 g ....

v 2500 J ....   **vi** 250 Pa ....

Maths focus 3: Writing numbers in a required form

Sometimes in chemistry you need to write a number in a particular form.

When very large or very small numbers are written using a power of ten, the standard way of doing this is to use a system called **standard form** or **standard index form** or **scientific notation**. A standard system is a system that can be understood by scientists in different laboratories and even different countries.

A number in standard form is expressed as a number greater than or equal to 1, but less than 10, multiplied by a power of ten. For example, 54 000 can be written as 5.4×10^4. However, 54×10^3 is *not* in standard form because 54 is not between 1 and 10.

The results of calculations should be rounded up or down to an appropriate number of **significant figures (sf)**. **Rounding** a number provides an approximation that uses fewer significant figures than the original number.

If something is significant, it is important. A number written to two significant figures shows the first two and therefore the most important digits. In chemistry the results of calculations should be written to the same number of significant figures as the lowest number of significant figures of the measurements used in the calculation.

What maths skills do you need to be able to understand very large and very small numbers?

1	Writing numbers in standard form	•	Write the digits as a number that is greater than or equal to 1 and less than 10.
		•	Work out how many times you need to multiply or divide the number by 10 to get to your original number.
		•	Write the number, using the correct power of ten.
2	Writing numbers to the required number of significant figures	•	Identify the correct number of significant figures.
		•	Decide whether to round up or down.

Maths skills practice

KEY WORDS

accuracy: how close a value is to the true value

decimal place: the place-value position of a number after a decimal point; the number 6.357 has three decimal places

estimate: (find) an approximate value

How does writing numbers in a required form help you to communicate numbers in chemistry?

Standard form helps you compare very small and large numbers. The power of ten gives a useful **estimate** of the size of the number.

It is important that all values in chemistry are recorded to an appropriate number of significant figures. For example, a student does a calculation that contains measurements to three significant figures. The student writes the result of the calculation as $34.938475\,cm^3$. The student's answer suggests a much greater degree of **accuracy** than was achieved in the experiment.

Maths skill 1: Writing numbers in standard form

KEY WORDS

decimal point: a symbol (dot) used in a decimal number that separates a whole number and its fractional part

A number in standard form always includes a number that is greater than or equal to 1, but less than 10, multiplied by a power of ten. Another way of thinking about this is that in standard form the **decimal point** always comes after the most significant figure.

So, for the number 4 060 000:

- 4.06×10^6 is in correct standard form because 4.06 is between 1 and 10.

- 406×10^4 is in index form, but it is *not* in standard form because 406 is greater than 10.

Standard form on your calculator

Calculators do not all work in the same way, so you must make sure you know how to use your calculator. This is especially important when you need to enter or read numbers in standard form. This may involve using the the 10^x key. On some calculators you need to use the E key (or the [EE] key). E is short for the mathematical term 'exponent' (another name for the index).

For example, to enter 1.67×10^{11}, a typical key sequence (the order in which the keys are pressed) would be:

1.67 10^x 11 or 1.67 E11

The screen would show the number as in Figure 1.3.

Figure 1.3: The number 1.67×10^{11} shown on a calculator.

WORKED EXAMPLE 1.8

12 g of carbon contains 6.02×10^{23} carbon atoms.

Use your calculator to work out how many carbon atoms there are in 24 g of carbon.

2×6.02 10^x 23 or 2×6.02 E23

WORKED EXAMPLE 1.9

Large numbers

Write 5 400 000 in standard form.

Step 1: Rewrite the non-zero digits as a number that is greater than or equal to 1 and less than 10.

5.4

CONTINUED

Step 2: Work out how many times you need to multiply this number by 10 to get your original number (Figure 1.4).

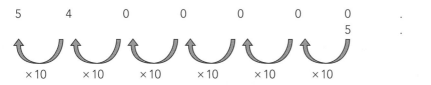

Figure 1.4: Working out how many times you have to multiply 5.4 by 10 to reach 5 400 000.

5.4 must be multiplied by 10 six times
$(5.4 \times 10 \times 10 \times 10 \times 10 \times 10 \times 10)$ to reach 5 400 000.

Step 3: Write the number, using the correct power of ten.

$$5.4 \times 10 \times 10 \times 10 \times 10 \times 10 \times 10 = 5.4 \times 10^6$$

> ### LOOK OUT
>
> If there are significant zeros between the digits in a number, these must appear in the number written in standard form, for example,
> $3\,050\,000 = 3.05 \times 10^6$

You can also use standard form to write very small numbers. For this you use negative powers of ten. The method for converting very small numbers into standard form is slightly different.

WORKED EXAMPLE 1.10

Small numbers

Write 0.000 001 2 in standard form.

Step 1: Rewrite the non-zero digits as a number that is greater or equal to 1 and less than 10.

1.2

Step 2: Work out how many times you need to divide this number by 10 to get your original number (Figure 1.5).

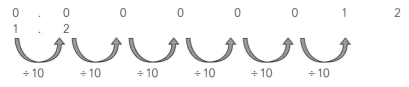

Figure 1.5: Working out how many times you have to divide 1.2 by 10 to get back to 0.000 001 2.

> CONTINUED

1.2 must be divided by 10 six times
$(1.2 \div 10 \div 10 \div 10 \div 10 \div 10 \div 10)$ to get back
to 0.0000012

Step 3: Write the number, using the correct power of ten.

$$1.2 \div 10 \div 10 \div 10 \div 10 \div 10 \div 10 = 1.2 \times \frac{1}{10 \times 10 \times 10 \times 10 \times 10 \times 10}$$

$$= 1.2 \times 10^{-6}$$

Questions

17 Write these numbers in standard form.

a   134 000   ....   b   103 000   ....

c   120 000 000   ....   d   140   ....

18 Write these values in standard form. Then, describe to your partner how you worked out the answer.

a   34 000 000 000 000 carbon atoms   b   142 000 g   ....

....   c   145 m^3 ....

19 Write these numbers in standard form.

a   0.0034   ....   b   0.0000054   ....

c   0.000 507   ....   d   0.000 000 009 754   ....

20 Write these measurements in standard form.

a   0.000 000 000 15 m   ....   b   0.003 g   ....

c   0.000 000 023 g   ....   d   0.0009 m^3 ....

21 Convert these measurements into metres. Write the measurements in standard form.

a   i   9 nm   ii   92 nm   ....

iii   6 μm   iv   73 μm   ....

b   Explain to your partner why some measurements were easy to convert to standard form and why other measurements were more difficult to convert to standard form.

Maths skill 2: Writing numbers to the required number of significant figures

The rules for rounding to a given number of significant figures are similar to the rules for rounding to the nearest 10 or 100 or to a given number of **decimal places**. The significant figures in a number are counted from the first non-zero digit.

WORKED EXAMPLE 1.11

Large numbers

Write 124 321 correct to two significant figures.

Step 1: Identify the correct number of significant figures.

The first two significant figures (sf) are the first and second digits in the number, which have the two highest place values. These are the two digits on the left of the digit to be rounded.

```
1st sf   2nd sf
  ↓        ↓
  1        2        4        3        2        1
```

Step 2: Decide whether to round up or down.

Look at the digit in the third significant place.

If the third digit is 0, 1, 2, 3 or 4, leave the first two digits as they are and replace all the other digits in the number with 0.

If the third digit is 5, 6, 7, 8 or 9, increase the digit in the second place by 1 and replace all the other digits in the number with 0.

The next digit is 4 so round down, giving 120 000.

WORKED EXAMPLE 1.12

Small numbers

Write 0.267 93 correct to two significant figures.

Step 1: Identify the correct number of significant figures.

Identify the first two significant figures (sf). The third figure is the one to be rounded.

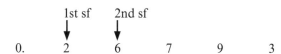

```
         1st sf   2nd sf
           ↓        ↓
  0.       2        6        7        9        3
```

Step 2: Decide whether to round up or down.

Look at the digit in the next place.

The next digit is 7, so round up the second significant figure.

This gives 0.27.

Questions

22 a Round 423 912 atoms to:

    i 1 sf ....   ii 3 sf ....

   b Round 1 064 126 atoms to:

    i 2 sf ....   ii 3 sf ....

23 a Round a mass of 0.324 g to:

    i 1 sf ....   ii 2 sf ....

   b Round a mass of 0.417 312 g to:

    i 1 sf ....   ii 2 sf ....

EXAM-STYLE QUESTIONS

1 The table shows the atomic radius of atoms for elements in Group I (alkali metals) of the Periodic Table.

Element (symbol)	Atomic radius / m
lithium (Li)	0.000 000 000 152
sodium (Na)	0.000 000 000 186
potassium (K)	0.000 000 000 231
rubidium (Rb)	0.000 000 000 244

   a **Describe** the pattern in atomic radius going down Group I.

   ....

   .... [2]

   b The atomic radius of caesium is about 0.000 000 000 1 m greater than rubidium. Estimate the atomic radius of caesium. **Give** your answer in standard form.

   .... [1]

                                                                    [Total: 3]

COMMAND WORDS

describe: state the points of a topic / give characteristics and main features

give: produce an answer from a given source or recall / memory

CONTINUED

2 A student measures the dimensions of a cuboid block of aluminium.

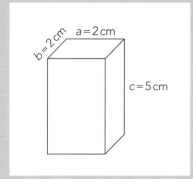

a Give each length in metres.

....

.... [3]

b i **Calculate** the volume of the cuboid ($a \times b \times c$) using the lengths in metres.

.... [2]

ii Give the volume in standard form.

.... [1]

The mass of the cuboid was measured as 0.054 kg.

c i Calculate the density of the cuboid.

$$\text{density} = \frac{\text{mass}}{\text{volume}}$$

....

.... [2]

ii Give the density rounded to one significant figure.

.... [1]

[Total: 9]

3 Beaker **A** contains 12 g of carbon. Beaker **B** contains 1.2 g of magnesium.

a Beaker **A** contains 602 000 000 000 000 000 000 000 atoms of carbon.

Give this number in standard form.

.... [1]

COMMAND WORD
calculate: work out from given facts, figures or information

CONTINUED

b A magnesium atom has a mass two times greater than the mass of a carbon atom.

    i Calculate how many grams of magnesium contain the same number of atoms as 12 g of carbon.

    ....

    .... [1]

    ii Calculate the number of atoms in 12 g of magnesium. Write your answer in standard form.

    ....

    .... [2]

    iii Calculate the number of atoms of magnesium in beaker **B**. Write your answer in standard form.

    ....

    .... [2]

[Total: 6]

> Chapter 2

> Working with data

WHY DO YOU NEED TO WORK WITH DATA IN CHEMISTRY?

- You can discover more about chemistry by making observations.

- Your observations may be a description. Descriptions are called qualitative data because they describe a quality (such as a colour change).

- Your observations may be measurements. Measurements are called quantitative data because they measure a quantity. Quantitative data are numbers. Sometimes this is called numerical data.

- The value of a measurement always has some uncertainty. You cannot be sure that the measurement is exactly correct.

Maths focus 1: Collecting data

KEY WORDS

meniscus: the curved surface of a liquid, for example in a tube or cylinder

qualitative data: data that are descriptive and not numerical

quantitative data: data that are numerical

uncertainty: range of variation in experimental results because of sources of error; the true value is expected to be within this range

Measurements can give you information about a reaction at the beginning and at the end of the reaction, and even how the quantities change during a reaction.

Measuring equipment that you use to collect data can be either digital or non-digital.

• Digital measuring equipment displays the measurement directly on a small screen. An electronic balance, pH meter, digital timer and temperature probe (Figure 2.1a) are all examples of digital equipment.

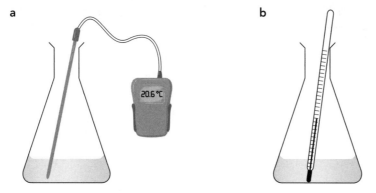

Figure 2.1 a: Digital thermometer. **b:** Non-digital thermometer.

• Non-digital equipment uses a scale. A scale is made up of equally spaced divisions with numbers marked at regular intervals. These numbers usually increase in values of 1, 2, 5 or 10. You read the measurement from the scale. A ruler, measuring cylinder, pipette and burette are all examples of non-digital equipment. Some thermometers are non-digital (Figure 2.1b).

The number of decimal places that you use when recording a measurement gives information about the level of **uncertainty** of the measurement. For example, a temperature recorded on a non-digital thermometer as 24 °C could actually be 24.2 °C or 23.8 °C. A temperature recorded with no decimal places (such as 24 °C) therefore shows greater uncertainty than a temperature recorded to one decimal place (such as 24.5 °C).

> **LOOK OUT**
>
> Always read a scale carefully so that you do not add to the uncertainty of the measurement.

What maths skills do you need to collect data?

1	Reading scales	• For a measuring cylinder, find the level of the liquid.
		• Read the largest number before this level on the scale.
		• Count the small divisions between this and the level of liquid.
		• Calculate the volume shown by each small division.
		• Add the volume shown by the number of small divisions to the larger number on the scale.
2	Recording to the correct number of decimal places	• Write down the reading of the scale division that is exactly at, or just before, the level when reading from small to large on the scale.
		• Decide whether the level is nearer the marked scale division or the half-way point between divisions and record the number correctly.

Maths skills practice

How does collecting data help you to understand reactions?

Marble is a type of rock composed of calcium carbonate. When small pieces of marble ('marble chips') are added to dilute hydrochloric acid, the reaction produces a gas (Figure 2.2). Think about the two different types of data you could collect from this experiment.

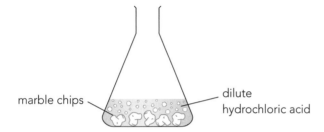

Figure 2.2: The reaction of marble chips with dilute hydrochloric acid.

You could write a description of the reaction. This is **qualitative data**. A description may help you to understand more about the reactants and products. For example, you could *describe* how the size of the marble chips gradually gets smaller as the calcium carbonate reacts.

You could collect **quantitative data**. Quantitative (numerical) data gives you more information about the reaction. For example, you could *measure* the volume of gas produced every 30 seconds (Figure 2.3) until the reaction stops.

Numerical data can be plotted on a graph. A graph could show how the volume of gas produced increases during the reaction.

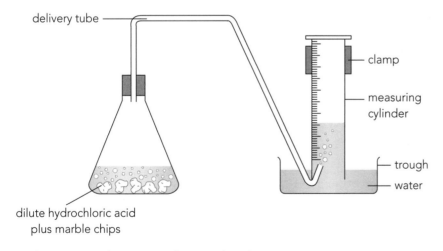

Figure 2.3: Measuring the amount of gas produced.

Maths skill 1: Reading scales

WORKED EXAMPLE 2.1

Figure 2.4 shows part of a $10\,cm^3$ measuring cylinder containing a liquid. Read the volume of liquid shown on the scale.

Figure 2.4: Part of a $10\,cm^3$ measuring cylinder containing a liquid.

Step 1: Find the level of the liquid.

Always read the measurement from the bottom of the **meniscus** (Figure 2.5).

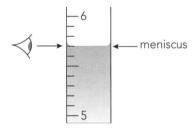

Figure 2.5: Always read the level of the liquid from the bottom of the meniscus.

Step 2: Read the *largest* number before this level on the scale.

The largest number on the scale, below the meniscus, is 5.

Step 3: Count the small divisions above this number, to the level of liquid.

The meniscus of the liquid is 7 small divisions above 5.

Step 4: Calculate the volume shown by each small division.

There are 10 small divisions between 5 and 6, so each division is equal to $0.1\,cm^3$.

Step 5: Add the volume shown by the number of small divisions to the larger number on the scale.

The meniscus of the liquid is 7 small divisions above the 5, so the total volume of liquid is: $5 + (7 \times 0.1) = 5.7$

Do not forget to give the correct units.

The volume is $5.7\,cm^3$.

> **LOOK OUT**
>
> The surface of the liquid in the measuring cylinder is curved. The curved surface is called the meniscus.

Questions

1   The thermometers in Figure 2.6 are marked in degrees Celsius (°C).

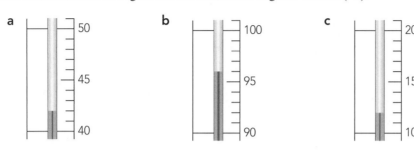

Figure 2.6: Parts of three thermometers marked in degrees Celsius (°C).

Read the temperature on each thermometer. Record your answers.

a   ....   b   c   ....

2   The measuring cylinders in Figure 2.7 are marked in cubic centimetres (cm^3).
    The scales on the measuring cylinders are different.

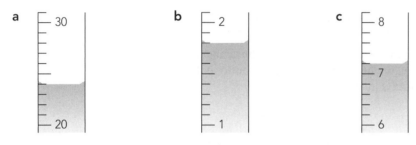

Figure 2.7: Three measuring cylinders marked in cubic centimetres (cm^3).

Read the volume of liquid in each measuring cylinder. Record your answers.

a   ....   b   c   ....

3   Work in pairs.

a   Look at the diagrams of a measuring cylinder and a burette in Figure 2.8.

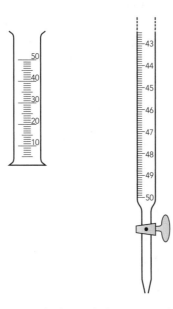

Figure 2.8: A measuring cylinder and a burette marked in cubic centimetres (cm³).

i   Discuss the difference between the scale on the measuring cylinder and the scale on the burette. How might the difference help you to make different types of measurements in an experiment?

....

....

....

ii   Describe how you read the scale on a burette differently.

....

....

....

b   The burettes in Figure 2.9 are marked in cubic centimetres (cm³).

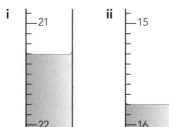

Figure 2.9: Two burettes are marked in cubic centimetres (cm³).

Read the volume of liquid in each burette. Record your answers.

i   ii   ....

c   Check your partner's answers. Did your partner remember to read the burette scale differently to how they read the measuring cylinder scale?

Maths skill 2: Recording to the correct number of decimal places

A more accurate measurement is closer to the true value.

The smallest change that you can measure with a non-digital thermometer is half a division. For a thermometer with divisions marked every 1 °C, the smallest change you can measure is therefore 0.5 °C.

You should record measurements from a thermometer correct to one decimal place, for example, 24.0 °C not 24 °C (Figure 2.10). This shows that there is less uncertainty in the measurement than simply recording the temperature to the nearest whole number (no decimal places).

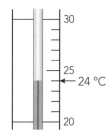

Figure 2.10: Record measurements from a thermometer to one decimal place (e.g. 24.0 °C).

On a burette, the smallest divisions are marked every 0.1 cm³. Burettes can also be read to the nearest half division (0.05 cm³). You should record burette measurements to two decimal places (Figure 2.11).

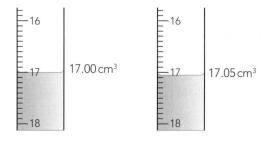

Figure 2.11: Record measurements from a burette to two decimal places.

WORKED EXAMPLE 2.2

Record the thermometer reading shown in Figure 2.12 to the correct number of decimal places.

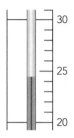

Figure 2.12: Record the thermometer reading.

Step 1: Write down the reading of the scale division that is exactly at, or just before, the level when reading from small to large on the scale.

Key questions to ask yourself:

- Does the scale read from top to bottom, or bottom to top, of the measuring instrument? The scale on a thermometer reads from bottom to top. The numbers increase going *up* the thermometer.

   The scale on a burette reads from top to bottom. The numbers increase going *down* the burette.

- Is the scale division just below or just above the level of the liquid? In this case, you need to read the division that is exactly at, or just below, the level. This division is 24.

   On a burette you need to read the division that is exactly at, or just above, the level of the liquid.

Step 2: Decide whether the level is nearer the marked scale division or the half-way point between divisions and record the number correctly.

If the reading level is closer to the marked division, write 0 at the end of the number. Remember to add a decimal point if necessary.

If the level is closer to the half-way point between divisions, write 5 at the end of the number. Remember to add a decimal point if necessary.

Always remember to give the correct units.

This reading is nearer the half-way point.

This reading should be written: $24.5\,°C$

Questions

4 Write down the temperature shown on each thermometer in Figure 2.13.
Give your answer to the correct number of decimal places.

a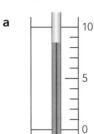

b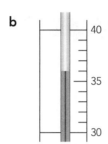

c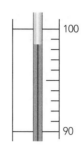

Figure 2.13: Write down the temperature shown on each thermometer.

a ....   **b** ....   **c** ....

5 Work in pairs. Mix some hot and cold water in a beaker. Ask your partner to use a thermometer to measure the temperature of the water.

Check your partner's answer. Have they read the temperature scale to the nearest half of a division?

Now swap roles and repeat the exercise.

6 Write down the volume shown on each burette in Figure 2.14. Give your answer to the correct number of decimal places.

a

b

c

Figure 2.14: Write down the volume shown on each burette.

a ....   **b** ....   **c** ....

d Check your answers. Did you remember to read the scale from top to bottom?

Maths focus 2: Understanding types of data

KEY WORDS

bar chart: a chart with separated rectangular bars of equal width; the height (or length) of a bar represents the value of the variable

categorical data: data that can be grouped into categories (types) but not ordered

continuous data: data that can take any numerical value within a range

controlled variable: a variable that is kept constant in an investigation

dependent variable: the variable that is measured or observed in an investigation, when the independent variable is changed

discrete data: data that can take only certain values

independent variable: the variable in an investigation that is changed by the experimenter

line graph: a graph of one variable against another where the data points fall on or close to a single line, which may be straight, curved or straight-line segments between points, depending on the relationship between the variables

range: the interval between the lowest value and the highest value, for example, of a measured variable or on the scale of a measuring instrument

trend: a pattern shown by data; on a graph this may be shown by points following a 'trend line', the best estimate of this being the best-fit line

x-axis: The line that is arranged from left to right on a graph; also known as the horizontal axis

y-axis: the line that is arranged from top to bottom on a graph; also known as the vertical axis

The type of data produced in an experiment depends on the design of the experiment. Usually there is one **independent variable** and one **dependent variable**.

- The independent variable is the variable that you *change* each time.

- The dependent variable is the variable that you *measure* each time.

LOOK OUT

Variables that remain constant during an experiment are known as **controlled variables**.

There are three different types of data:

- Some data can be sorted into categories (groups), but the categories cannot be easily ordered, for example, the names of different metals. This type of data is known as **categorical data**.

- Sometimes the numerical data can take any value within a certain **range**, for example, the temperature of an object. This type of data is known as **continuous data**.

- Occasionally, numerical data can only take certain values, for example, the numbers of protons in an atom can only be whole numbers. This type of data is known as **discrete data**.

What maths skills do you need to understand different types of data?

1	Identifying the independent and dependent variables	• Identify the variable that is changed during the experiment (the independent variable).
		• Identify the variable that is measured when the independent variable is changed (the dependent variable).
2	Distinguishing categorical, continuous and discrete data	• Decide if the independent variable is recorded as words or numbers.
		• Decide if numerical data can take on any value in a range or only certain values.

Maths skills practice

How does understanding different types of data help you to decide what type of graph to draw?

- It is important to draw the correct type of chart or graph for the data that is being recorded. If the independent variable is categorical, draw a **bar chart**.

- If the independent variable is continuous, draw a **line graph**. On a line graph, the line between the plotted points may be used to find other values..

> **LOOK OUT**
>
> Always plot the independent variable on the **x-axis** (horizontal axis) and plot the dependent variable on the **y-axis** (vertical axis).

Maths skill 1: Identifying independent and dependent variables

WORKED EXAMPLE 2.3

A student adds some marble chips to hydrochloric acid and measures the temperature every 30 seconds for 5 minutes. Write down the independent variable and the dependent variable.

Step 1: Identify the variable that is *changed* during the experiment. This is the independent variable.

The student measures the temperature every 30 seconds, so the independent variable is time.

Step 2: Identify the variable that is *measured* when the independent variable is changed. This is the dependent variable.

The student measures the temperature every 30 seconds, so the dependent variable is temperature.

LOOK OUT

Sometimes a description of an experiment gives the units but not the name of the variable. You need to remember that measuring in cubic centimetres (cm^3) means that the variable is *volume* or that measuring in grams (g) means that the variable is *mass*.

Questions

7 Work in pairs. Read the following description of an experiment:

A student adds $10\,cm^3$ of acid, $1\,cm^3$ at a time, to a beaker containing an alkali. She uses a pH meter to measure the pH after the addition of each portion of acid.

a Sketch a diagram to show the experiment. This will help you to visualise the experiment.

b Discuss with your partner what you think is changed during the experiment. Write down your answer. This is the independent variable.

....

c Then discuss what you think is measured during the experiment. Write down your answer. This is the dependent variable.

....

8   Identify the independent variable and the dependent variable for each of the
     following experiments.

   a   A student adds some marble chips to a flask containing acid. She measures
        the mass every 30 seconds for 5 minutes.

        i   Dependent variable: ii   Independent variable: ....

   b   A student adds sodium thiosulfate to hydrochloric acid and measures
        the time it takes for the solution to turn cloudy. The student repeats the
        experiment at four different temperatures.

        i   Dependent variable: ii   Independent variable: ....

   c   A student uses a pH meter to test the pH of five different solutions.

        i   Dependent variable: ii   Independent variable: ....

   d   A scientist determines the melting points of elements with different atomic
        numbers. The scientist is trying to find a **trend** between the atomic number
        and the melting point.

        i   Dependent variable: ii   Independent variable: ....

   e   How did you decide the independent and the dependent variable for each
        experiment? What factors did you think about?

   ....

   ....

   ....

   ....

Maths skill 2: Distinguishing categorical, continuous and discrete data

WORKED EXAMPLE 2.4

A student adds some zinc powder to copper sulfate solution. The student
measures the temperature every 30 seconds for 5 minutes. Write down whether
the independent variable is categorical, continuous or discrete.

Step 1: Decide if the independent variable is recorded as words or numbers.

         If it is recorded in words, then the data are categorical.

         In this case, the data are numerical, so a further decision needs to be made.

Step 2: Decide if the numerical data can take on any value in a range or only
         certain values.

         The independent variable is time.

CONTINUED

The student has chosen to measure the temperature after 30 seconds, 60 seconds, 90 seconds, and so on, for 5 minutes. However, the temperature could be measured at 10 seconds or 7 seconds or at any other time. The independent variable is therefore continuous.

Numerical data that can only be certain values are discrete data. The number of protons in atoms of each element is always a whole number.

Questions

9   Work in pairs. Read the following description of an experiment:

A student adds 0.5 g of small-sized marble chips to a conical flask and adds hydrochloric acid (Figure 2.15). The student measures the time it takes for all of the marble chips to react. The student repeats the experiment with medium- and large-sized marble chips.

small marble chips   medium marble chips   large marble chips

Figure 2.15: Set-up to measure the time taken for different-sized marble chips to react.

a   Decide with your partner what the independent variable is. Is it described in words or numbers? Write down your answer.

....

b   Is the independent variable a categorical, continuous or discrete variable?

....

10 Read the descriptions of the experiments in question **8** again. Write down whether each independent variable is categorical, continuous or discrete.

a   ....   b   ....

c   ....   d   ....

e   Check your answers to **a**, **b**, **c** and **d** by ticking the boxes in the checklist:

Are categorical variables represented by words?   ☐

Can continuous variables be measured for values in between those chosen?   ☐

Can discrete variables only be certain values?   ☐

Maths focus 3: Recording and processing data

KEY WORDS

formula (mathematical): an equation that shows the relationship between variables

mean: an average value: the sum of a set of values divided by the number of values in the set

precision: the closeness of agreement between several measured values obtained by repeated measurements; the precision of a single value can be indicated by the number of significant figures given in the number, for example 4.027 has greater precision (is more precise) than 4.0

processed data: data produced by calculation using raw experimental data

random error: measurement error that varies in an unpredictable way from one measurement to the next

raw data: data collected by measurement or observation

systematic error: measurement error that results in measured values differing from the true value by the same amount each time a measurement is made; this may occur for example when a balance reads 0.02 g with no mass on it

Recording data helps to communicate measurements clearly to other people. It also helps you to process the data. You can use maths to calculate the **mean** (average) and other quantities.

Recording data clearly in a table makes it easier to plot a graph. A graph helps you to identify any patterns or trends in the data.

Figure 2.16a shows data recorded in an unorganised way. The units are not always used and the measurements are not presented in order.

a
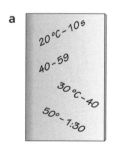

b
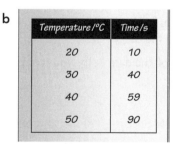

Temperature /°C	Time /s
20	10
30	40
40	59
50	90

Figure 2.16 a: Unorganised data. **b:** Organised data.

LOOK OUT

Data that show a trend show an increase or decrease in the dependent variable as the independent variable is increased.

Figure 2.16b shows the data recorded in a table. The units are the same throughout and the measurements are presented in a systematic (organised) way. This makes it easy to see any patterns or trends in the data. The organised data clearly show that there is a trend in the data: as the temperature increases, the time also increases.

What maths skills do you need to record and process data?

1	Drawing tables	• Work out how many columns and rows are needed.
		• Draw the table.
		• Add a heading to each column. Include a unit if required.
		• Add the values of the independent variable.
2	Drawing tables to help process data	• Work out how many extra columns you need.
		• Draw the table.
3	Recording processed data to an appropriate number of significant figures	• Use a calculator to complete any calculations.
		• Note the smallest number of significant figures that occurs in the data.
		• Round the calculated values to this number of significant figures.

Maths skills practice

How does recording and processing data help you to understand chemistry?

Drawing a table helps you to present data so that it is easy to read. A well-organised table helps you to communicate data.

Using a table also helps to organise data, making it easier to plot a graph. A graph makes it easier to identify patterns and trends in the data.

Processing the data to calculate the mean value of the data helps you to ensure there is less uncertainty in the data.

Maths skill 1: Drawing tables

Record the independent variable in the left-hand column of a table, and record the dependent variable in the right-hand column.

For categorical data, add words to describe the categories for the independent variable in the left-hand column. For continuous and discrete data, add numerical values for the independent variable in the left-hand column. You can do this before you start an experiment.

> **LOOK OUT**
>
> A pattern in the data can show a repeating trend where the dependent variable is highest at regular intervals (such as levels of pollution at the same time each day).

Add any numerical data you record for the dependent variable in the right-hand column.

You can also use a table to record **qualitative data**. In this case, record your observations in the right-hand column.

WORKED EXAMPLE 2.5

A student pours $20\,cm^3$ of hydrochloric acid into a polystyrene cup and measures its temperature. The student then adds a spatula of powdered magnesium metal to the acid and uses a digital thermometer to measure the temperature every 10 seconds for 1 minute. Draw a table to record her data.

Step 1: Work out how many columns and rows are needed.

The student needs two columns: one column for the independent variable and one column for the dependent variable.

The student measures the temperature at 0, 10, 20, 30, 40, 50 and 60 seconds (1 minute), so she needs one header row plus seven more rows in the table.

Step 2: Draw the table.

Step 3: Add the headings to each column.

Adding the unit symbol to the column heading means that you do not have to write the unit symbol after each number in the column.

Always remember to separate the name of the variable and its unit symbol with a '/' (solidus) sign.

The independent variable is time. Time has units of seconds (s).

The heading for the left-hand column is 'Time / s'.

The dependent variable is temperature. Temperature has units of degrees Celsius (°C). The heading for the right-hand column is 'Temperature / °C'.

Step 4: Add the values of the independent variable to the left-hand column.

Table 2.1 shows the final table.

Time / s	Temperature / °C
0	
10	
20	
30	
40	
50	
60	

Table 2.1: Final table to record the data (temperature).

Questions

11 Read the following descriptions of experiments **A** and **B**:

Experiment A

A student adds $5\,cm^3$ of acid, $1\,cm^3$ at a time, to a beaker containing an alkali. She uses a pH meter to measure the pH after the addition of each portion of acid.

Experiment B

A student adds some marble chips to a flask containing acid. He measures the mass, in grams, every 30 seconds for 2 minutes (120 seconds).

a **i** Draw a table for experiment **A**.   **ii** Draw a table for experiment **B**.

> **LOOK OUT**
>
> The pH scale does not have any units; it ranges from 0 to 14.

b Work in pairs. Check your partner's tables are correct by ticking the boxes in the checklist:

	Table **A**	Table **B**
Number of columns	☐	☐
Number of rows	☐	☐
Column headings	☐	☐
Units included in column heading (and /)	☐	☐

12 A student uses a pH meter to test the acidity or alkalinity of three different types of substance: A, B and C. Draw a table for this experiment.

13 Work in pairs. Read the following description of an experiment:

A student carries out flame tests on three different metal compounds (lithium chloride, sodium chloride and potassium chloride). She records the colour of the flame after each test.

Discuss with your partner how the table for recording the results will be similar to the table in question **12** and how it will be different when completed. Write down your answer.

....

....

....

....

....

....

Maths skill 2: Drawing tables to help process data

The original observations or measurements that you make are known as **raw data**.

Sometimes you need to apply mathematical processing to the raw data, for example:

- You may need to calculate the mean for each set of repeated data.

- You may have measured the mass and volume of different metals in order to calculate the density of the metals.

The results of the calculations are called **processed data**.

Recording both the raw data and processed data in a well-organised table can help to make calculations easier.

WORKED EXAMPLE 2.6

A student measures the time it takes 0.5 g of small marble chips to react with 50 cm³ of acid. He repeats the experiment two more times until he has a set of three measurements.

The student then carries out three similar experiments with medium marble chips and another three similar experiments with large marble chips.

Draw up a table that he could use to record these results and to calculate the mean.

Step 1: Work out how many columns are needed.

The student needs one column for the independent variable (size of marble chip). He must include a column for the three experiments for each chip size, so he needs three columns for the dependent variable (time in seconds). The student also needs an extra column to record the mean that he calculates.

The student needs a total of five columns in his table.

CONTINUED

Step 2: Draw the table, as described in Maths skill 1: Drawing tables.

Work out how many rows the student needs.

The student is testing three sizes of marble chip, so after the header row he needs three more rows.

Add the heading to each column.

The independent variable is the size of the marble chips. This does not have a unit.

There are three columns for the dependent variable (Time / s). This needs one overall heading at the top and three separate column headings (Test 1, Test 2 and Test 3) below (Table 2.2).

Time / s		
Test 1	Test 2	Test 3

Table 2.2: Column headings for the three test repeats.

The column on the right of the table should have the heading 'Mean', with the correct unit symbol of s for seconds. The units for the mean are the same as the units for the dependent variable.

Write the values of the independent variable that are going to be tested in the left-hand column. In this experiment, the independent variable is a categorical variable, so the words 'small', 'medium' and 'large' need to be added to the table.

Table 2.3 shows the final table.

Size of marble chip	Time / s			Mean time / s
	Test 1	Test 2	Test 3	
small				
medium				
large				

Table 2.3: Final table with columns for size of marble chip and mean time added.

> ### LOOK OUT
> The mean is calculated as the sum of a set of values divided by the number of values in the data set.

> ### LOOK OUT
> The units of the mean are always the same as the units of the data used to calculate the mean.

Questions

14 Read the following descriptions of experiments **A** and **B**:

Experiment A

A student adds sodium thiosulfate solution to hydrochloric acid at 20 °C and measures the time it takes for the solution to turn cloudy. She carries out the experiment two more times.

The student then performs the experiment three times at 30 °C and three times at 40 °C. She calculates the mean time taken for the solution to turn cloudy for each temperature.

Experiment B

A student adds 1 g of small marble chips to hydrochloric acid in a conical flask. The student uses a gas syringe to measure the volume of carbon dioxide produced in 30 seconds. He carries out the experiment two more times.

The student then performs the experiment three times with medium marble chips and three times with large marble chips. He calculates the mean volume of gas produced for each size of chip.

a **i** Draw a table for experiment **A** that clearly displays the data and the mean.

  ii Draw a table for experiment **B** that clearly displays the data and the mean.

b Work in pairs. Describe to your partner how your tables help you to calculate the mean.

15 A student is investigating the density of four pieces of metal (copper, iron aluminium and tin). The student measures the volume and mass of each piece of metal and records the data in a table. She then calculates the density, using the **formula**: density $= \dfrac{\text{mass}}{\text{volume}}$.

   a Draw a table to clearly display the data.

   b Check your table. Do the mass and volume appear in the correct order to help you to calculate the density?

Maths skill 3: Recording processed data to the correct number of significant figures

Almost every measurement has some degree of error or uncertainty.

An awareness of accuracy and sources of error is important in evaluating the results of an experiment and for suggesting ways in which the methods used in an investigation could be improved.

There are different reasons why measurements have some uncertainty.

Accuracy is a measure of how close the measured value is to the true value. The accuracy of the results depends on the measuring apparatus used and the skill of the person taking the measurements.

When you process experimental data, the number of significant figures in your answer should be the same as the smallest number of significant figures used in the data values.

You must not use more significant figures in your final calculated answer because this would indicate that your measurements were more precise then they actually were and suggest a higher degree of accuracy than was actually achieved.

See Chapter 1, Maths focus 3, Maths skill 2 for more information about writing numbers to the correct number of significant figures.

Random errors often occur when you are carrying out an experiment. Working out the mean of repeated measurements reduces uncertainty due to random errors.

Repeated results that are close together indicate that the data have **precision**. However, even if results are in close agreement this does not necessarily mean that the data values are accurate. There could be a **systematic error** that is making all the data slightly too large or too small. An example of a systematic error could be a zeroing error on a balance. A zeroing error occurs if the balance gives a reading when the mass should be zero.

WORKED EXAMPLE 2.7

A student measures the volume of carbon dioxide produced during a reaction. Calculate the mean volume of the three measurements in Table 2.4. Record your answer to the correct number of significant figures.

Volume / cm³		
Test 1	Test 2	Test 3
22.4	22.2	21.8

Table 2.4: Volume of carbon dioxide produced during a reaction.

Step 1: Use a calculator to complete any calculations.

Calculate the mean:

$$\frac{22.4 + 22.2 + 21.8}{3} = 22.1333$$

Step 2: Note the lowest number of significant figures in the data.

Each measurement has three significant figures.

Step 3: Round the calculated value to this number of significant figures.

22.1 cm³

> **LOOK OUT**
>
> A reading that is very different to the other readings is called an anomalous result. If you can explain why the measurement is so different (e.g. due to an error in the experiment) then it should be ignored when calculating the mean.

Questions

16 A student measured the time it took for a reaction to produce 20 cm³ of hydrogen gas. The student performed the experiment three times. The results are shown in Table 2.5.

Time / s		
Test 1	Test 2	Test 3
16	17	17

Table 2.5: Time taken for a reaction to produce 20 cm³ of hydrogen gas.

a   Calculate the mean time. Write the answer shown on your calculator.

....

b   Write the answer to an appropriate number of significant figures.

....

> **LOOK OUT**
>
> If time is measured in minutes and seconds, change the time into seconds before finding the mean. 1 minute = 60 seconds.

17 A student measured how much the mass of a reactant decreased during a reaction. The student calculated the mass lost after 10 seconds. The experiment was performed three times. The results are shown in Table 2.6.

Loss of mass / g		
Test 1	Test 2	Test 3
1.24	1.27	1.23

Table 2.6: Loss of mass of a reactant after 10 seconds.

a Calculate the mean loss of mass. Write the answer shown on your calculator.

....

b Write the answer to an appropriate number of significant figures.

....

18 A student used a burette to measure the volume of acid required to neutralise an alkali. The student performed the experiment three times. The results are shown in Table 2.7.

Volume / cm³		
Test 1	Test 2	Test 3
20.05	20.10	19.95

Table 2.7: The volume of acid required to neutralise an alkali.

Calculate the mean result of the three experiments. Record the mean to an appropriate number of significant figures.

....

....

....

19 Check your partner's answers for questions 16, 17 and 18. Discuss with your partner why each answer is recorded to a different number of significant figures. Write down your explanation.

....

....

....

....

LOOK OUT

Loss of mass is an example of processed data. The raw data is simply the mass.

Loss of mass equals original mass minus mass at a given time.

EXAM-STYLE QUESTIONS

1   A student investigated the density of three small samples of different metals (iron, aluminium and copper). The student used the following method:

   •   Use a balance to find the mass of the metal sample.
   •   Add 5.0 cm³ of water to a measuring cylinder.
   •   Drop the metal sample into the measuring cylinder.
   •   Record the new volume.
   •   Calculate the density of the metal sample.
   •   Repeat the steps with the remaining two metal samples.

   a   Draw a table for the student to record her measurements and calculated value for density.

   [4]

   b   The diagram shows the measuring cylinder (cm³) and digital balance readings. Record the measurements in the table.

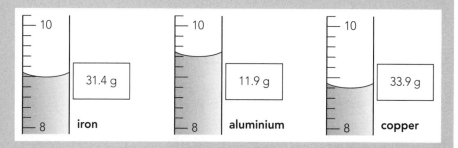

   [4]

COMMAND WORD

calculate: work out from given facts, figures or information

CONTINUED

c   **Calculate** the density of each metal. Record the density in the table to an appropriate number of significant figures.

....

....

.... **[4]**

[Total 12]

2   The temperature was measured during two different reactions: **A** (copper sulfate solution + zinc powder) and **B** (potassium nitrate + water). Each experiment was performed three times.

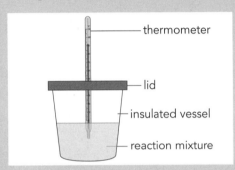

thermometer

lid

insulated vessel

reaction mixture

Reaction A: copper sulfate solution and zinc powder

a   Record the maximum temperature measurements in the table.

Test	Thermometer diagram	Maximum temperature of solution / °C	Temperature change / °C
1			
2			
3			

[3]

CONTINUED

b   The temperature of the solution was 23 °C at the start of each test. Calculate the temperature change for each test and record this in the table.   [3]

c   Calculate the mean temperature change for the copper sulfate + zinc reaction. Give your answer to the correct number of significant figures.

....

....

.... [2]

Reaction B: potassium nitrate + water

Test	Maximum temperature of solution / °C	Temperature change / °C
1	20.5	−2.5
2	20.0	−3.0
3	19.0	−4.0

d   Calculate the mean temperature change for the potassium nitrate + water reaction. Give your answer to the correct number of significant figures.

....

....

.... [2]

[Total 10]

Chapter 3

> Drawing charts and graphs

WHY DO YOU NEED TO DRAW CHARTS AND GRAPHS IN CHEMISTRY?

- Charts and graphs make it easier to compare data values and to look for patterns and relationships. A table is better for sharing actual values.

- Different types of chart and graph are used to display different types of data.

- The most common types of charts and graphs that you will use in chemistry are:

  - bar charts
  - pie charts
  - line graphs.

Maths focus 1: Drawing bar charts

A bar chart (also known as a bar graph) is useful for presenting and comparing categorical data. A bar chart consists of rectangular bars. The heights of the bars show the data values of different categories. For example, the bar chart shown in Figure 3.1 shows the number of grams of the most common elements found inside a smartphone. Some of the elements are found as the element (copper). Other elements are combined as compounds (silicon dioxide).

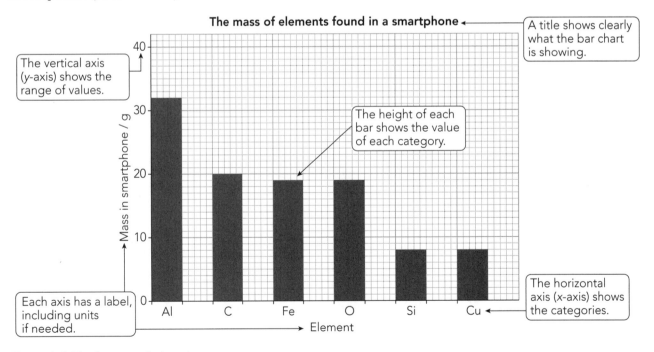

Figure 3.1: The features of a bar chart.

See Chapters 2 and 4 for more information about understanding different types of data and how different types of charts and graphs can be used to interpret data.

The graph paper you will use most often to draw charts and graphs will be made up of large, medium and small squares, as shown in Figure 3.2.

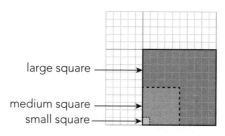

Figure 3.2: Typical graph paper

The scale on an axis tells you how much each square on the graph paper represents. The values are easier to read if each large square has a value of 1, 2, 5 or a multiple of a power of 10 of these numbers (e.g. 10, 20, 50 or 0.1, 0.2, 0.5).

What maths skills do you need to draw a bar chart?

1	Choosing a suitable scale for the vertical axis (y-axis)	• Find the maximum value needed on the y-axis. • Choose a scale that is easy to read and occupies at least half of the available space.
2	Drawing the bars	• Draw and label the axes. • Use the vertical scale to work out the heights of the bars. • Draw the bars with the same width, leaving a small gap between them.

Maths skills practice

How does drawing a bar chart help you to understand patterns in the properties of the elements?

Each chemical element has different properties. For example, each element has a different melting point, boiling point and density. Drawing a bar chart of data makes it easier to compare the properties and to see any trends or patterns.

LOOK OUT

Always use a bar chart if one of the variables (usually the independent variable) is not numerical. Discrete data can also be shown on a bar chart.

Maths skill 1: Choosing a suitable scale for the vertical axis (y-axis)

WORKED EXAMPLE 3.1

Table 3.1 shows the densities of some metal elements (rounded to one decimal place).

Element	Density / g per cm³
aluminium	2.7
copper	8.9
iron	7.9
gold	19.3

Table 3.1: Densities of different metal elements.

What scale should be used for the y-axis of a bar chart of this data? Assume the grid supplied for the bar chart has a height of five large squares.

Step 1: Find the *maximum* value needed on the y-axis.

The largest density value is $19.3 \, \text{g/cm}^3$. Rounding this up to the nearest whole number gives a maximum value of $20 \, \text{g/cm}^3$ on the y-axis.

Step 2: Choose a scale that is easy to read and occupies at least half of the available space (Table 3.2).

Scale (one large square represents)	Largest value that can be plotted	Do the data values fit?	Does the scale occupy more than half of the grid?
$1 \, \text{g/cm}^3$	$5 \, \text{g/cm}^3$	no	–
$2 \, \text{g/cm}^3$	$10 \, \text{g/cm}^3$	no	–
$5 \, \text{g/cm}^3$	$25 \, \text{g/cm}^3$	yes	yes

Table 3.2: Table to help work out the scale of the y-axis of a bar chart.

Therefore, using one large square to represent $5 \, \text{g/cm}^3$ is a suitable scale.

> **LOOK OUT**
>
> Remember that the plotted data must also occupy more than half the space.

Questions

1 Work in pairs. The data in Table 3.3 show the melting points of some elements in the third period (row) of the Periodic Table.

Element	Melting point / °C
sodium	98
magnesium	650
aluminium	660
silicon	1414

Table 3.3: Melting points of some elements in the third period of the Periodic Table.

Think about what scale should be used for the *y*-axis of a bar chart of this data.

a Look at the scales on the three axes **A**, **B** and **C** in Figure 3.3.

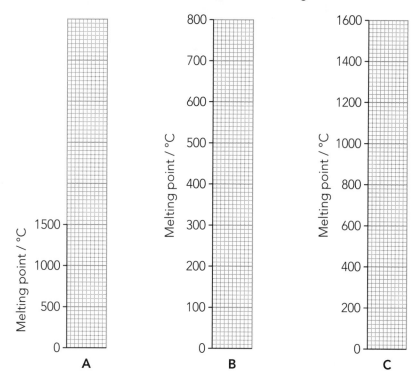

Figure 3.3: Three axes **A**, **B** and **C**.

Discuss the scale on each axis with your partner:

- Do the data values in Table 3.3 fit on the scale?
- Does the scale occupy more than half the height of the grid?

Which is the best scale to use? ....

b On this scale, what does one large square represent? ....°C

2   The data in Table 3.4 show the melting points of some Group I (alkali metal) elements (rounded to two significant figures).

Element	Melting point / °C
sodium	98
potassium	64
rubidium	39
caesium	29

Table 3.4: Melting points of some Group I (alkali metal) elements.

Think about what scale should be used for the *y*-axis of a bar chart of this data.

a   Complete the table to suggest three possible scales for a grid that has a height of three large squares.

Scale (one large square represents:)	Largest value that can be plotted	Do the data values fit?	Does the scale occupy more than half of the grid?
2°C			
20°C			
40°C			

b   Which is the best scale for the axis, and why?

....

Maths skill 2: Drawing the bars

WORKED EXAMPLE 3.2

The data in Table 3.5 show the densities of three different elements (rounded to one decimal place). Draw a bar chart to compare these densities. Use a scale of one large square to represent $1\,g/cm^3$ for the *y*-axis.

Element	Density / g per cm^3
aluminium	2.7
magnesium	1.7
lithium	0.5

Table 3.5: Densities of three different elements.

CONTINUED

Step 1: Draw and label the axes.

Remember that the categories (elements) are shown on the **x-axis** (horizontal axis) and the density is shown on the *y*-axis (vertical axis).

Step 2: Use the vertical scale to work out the heights of the bars (Figure 3.4).

To work out the value of each small square, divide the value of a large square by 10.

$$\frac{1}{10}\,g/cm^3 = 0.1\,g/cm^3$$

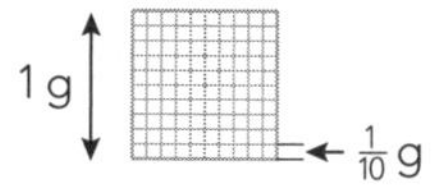

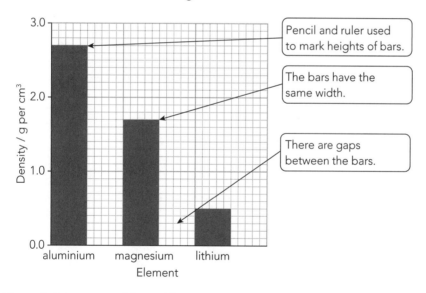

Figure 3.4: Value of each small square.

Step 3: Draw the bars.

Each of the bars should be the same width. Leave a small space between the bars.

The final bar chart is shown in Figure 3.5.

> Pencil and ruler used to mark heights of bars.

> The bars have the same width.

> There are gaps between the bars.

Figure 3.5: Densities of three different elements.

Questions

3   Draw a bar chart to compare the densities of the three Group I alkali metals in Table 3.6.

Element	Density / g per cm³
lithium	0.53
sodium	0.97
potassium	0.86

Table 3.6: Densities of three Group I alkali metals.

a   Draw and label the axes on the grid. Use a scale of one large square to represent $0.2\,\text{g}/\text{cm}^3$ on the *y*-axis.

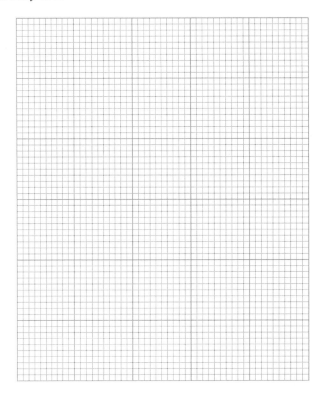

b   What does each small square on this axis represent?   ....

c   Draw the three bars on your chart.

4 Work in pairs. Table 3.7 shows the boiling point of five noble gases.

Element	Boiling point / °C
neon	−246
argon	−186
krypton	−153
xenon	−108
radon	−62

Table 3.7: Boiling points of five noble gases.

Think about the data values. Some of the values are negative values.

a Look at the scales on the three axes **A**, **B** and **C** in Figure 3.6.

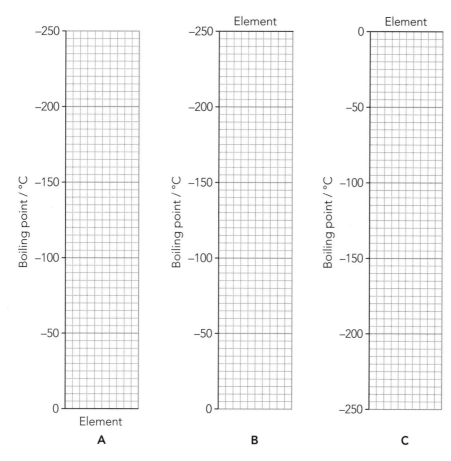

Figure 3.6: Three axes **A**, **B** and **C**.

Discuss which axis should be used for negative values.

The correctly drawn axis is ....

b Draw and label the axes on the grid.

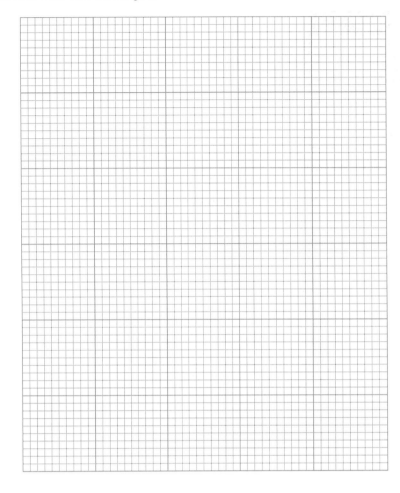

c **i** What does one large square represent on the *y*-axis? ....°C

ii What does each small square on the *y*-axis represent? ....°C

d Draw the five bars on your chart.

e Check your partner's graph. Does neon have a lower boiling point than argon?

LOOK OUT

On some scales, you will need to round your data values. For example, on a scale where 1 small square represents 1 °C, a temperature of 24.4 °C cannot be plotted exactly. You can only plot to the nearest half a small square. In this case you need to round the measurement to the nearest 0.5 °C and plot the point at 24.5 °C.

Maths focus 2: Drawing pie charts

In chemistry, **pie charts** are used less often than bar charts. A pie chart does not show the actual values of the data that you have measured.

A pie chart is a circular chart that helps you compare proportions or **percentages** of groups or categories that make up a whole. A pie chart cannot be used to show the percentage of carbon dioxide in a classroom every hour but it can be used to show the percentage of different gases that make up the whole atmosphere. Each of the separate categories of data is represented by a **sector** of the circle. For example, the sectors in the pie chart in Figure 3.7 show the percentages of different gases in the air.

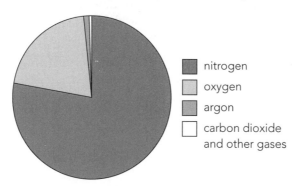

nitrogen

oxygen

argon

carbon dioxide and other gases

Figure 3.7: Percentages of different gases in the air.

The pie chart has been drawn with the sector for the category with the largest percentage starting at the top of the circle and being measured clockwise.

What maths skills do you need to draw a pie chart?

1	Converting percentages to angles	• Multiply each percentage by 3.6°.
		• Check that the angles add up to 360°.
2	Drawing the sectors	• List the categories in order of percentage, from largest to smallest.
		• Draw a circle with a vertical line from the centre of the circle to the edge of the circle.
		• Use a protractor to measure and mark the first angle, then draw the first line.
		• Move your protractor around so that it lies on this new line before measuring the next angle. Repeat for all of the angles.

Maths skills practice

How does drawing a pie chart help you to understand the composition of different alloys?

An alloy is a mixture of elements (usually metals) designed to have properties that are useful for a particular purpose. The properties of an alloy depend on its composition (percentage of different metals). The sectors on a pie chart can be used to show the percentages of each metal in the alloy mixture. This is a visual way of showing the composition of an alloy.

Maths skill 1: Converting percentages to angles

The total **angle** at the centre of a full circle is 360°. 1% is equal to 1 hundredth of a whole turn. So, 1% is represented by $\dfrac{360°}{100} = 3.6°$.

> ### WORKED EXAMPLE 3.3
>
> Brass alloy has a composition of 70% copper and 30% zinc. Calculate the angle for each sector of the pie chart to show the composition of brass.
>
> **Step 1:**   Multiply each percentage by 3.6° (Table 3.8).
>
>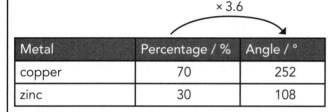
>
> | Metal | Percentage / % | Angle / ° |
> |---|---|---|
> | copper | 70 | 252 |
> | zinc | 30 | 108 |
>
> **Table 3.8:** The angles for each sector of a pie chart showing the percentage composition of brass.
>
> **Step 2:**   Check that the angles add up to 360°.
>
> $252° + 108° = 360°$
>
>   Sometimes you may need to round the angles to the nearest whole degree. Always check that the angles still add up to 360°.

Questions

5   Work in pairs. Bronze alloy has a typical composition of 90% copper and 10% tin.

   a   Discuss with your partner how you could work out the angles of the sectors in a pie chart to present this data. How many methods of calculating the angles can you think of?

   b   Use one method to calculate the angles. Record your answers in the following table.

Metal	Percentage / %	Angle / °
copper	90	
tin	10	

LOOK OUT

If you want to calculate the angles without using a calculator, remember that every 10% is represented by 36° in the pie chart. 50% is 180° and 25% is 90°.

Maths skill 2: Drawing the sectors

Amalgam is an alloy that can be used in dental fillings. The composition of amalgam is shown in Table 3.9.

Metal	Percentage / %	Angle / °
copper	10	36
mercury	50	180
silver	25	90
tin	15	54

Table 3.9: Composition of amalgam.

Draw a pie chart to show the composition of amalgam.

Step 1: List the categories in order of percentage, from largest to smallest.

mercury   50%   180°

silver   25%   90°

tin   15%   54°

copper   10%   36°

Step 2: Draw a circle and mark a point at the top of the circle.

Draw the first line vertically from the centre to this point (the **radius**) as shown in Figure 3.8.

Figure 3.8: The first step in drawing a pie chart is to draw a circle and a vertical line.

◄ CONTINUED

Step 3:   Use a protractor to measure and mark the first angle. Then draw the first line.

Place your protractor so that the base line of the protractor (the line through 0/180 at both ends and the centre) is aligned on the vertical line and the centre of the protractor is over the centre of the circle.

Measure and mark your first angle (180°). Be sure to choose the correct scale on the protractor. See Figure 3.9.

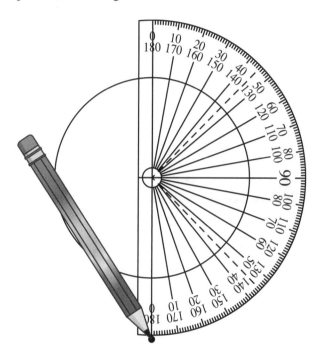

Figure 3.9: Using a protractor to measure the angle of the first sector in a pie chart.

Place your ruler so that it is aligned on the centre of the circle and the mark you have made for the first angle. Then draw the radius.

Step 4:   Move your protractor around so the base line of the protractor is aligned on the new line and the centre of the protractor is over the centre of the circle. Then measure the next angle.

Mark the angle and draw the radius to complete the second sector.

Move your protractor around so the base line is aligned on this new line and the centre is over the centre of the circle.

Measure and mark your next angle and draw the radius.

Repeat the previous process until you have drawn all the sectors.

As a check, measure the final angle to make sure it is correct (in this case 36°).

> **LOOK OUT**
>
> Draw the circle for a pie chart using a compass. The point of the compass will mark the centre of the circle.

CONTINUED

The final pie chart is shown in Figure 3.10.

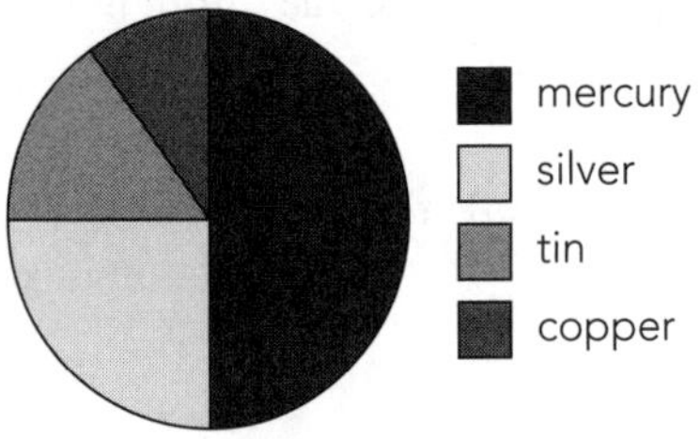

■ mercury
□ silver
▨ tin
▩ copper

Figure 3.10: The composition of amalgam.

LOOK OUT

Your final pie chart should include either labels or an appropriate key using different colours so that the categories represented by the sectors are clearly identified.

Questions

6 Solder is an alloy used to join two metals together. Table 3.10 shows the composition of one type of solder.

Metal	Percentage / %	Angle / °
tin	90	324
silver	5	18
copper	5	18

Table 3.10: Composition of solder.

Draw a pie chart to show the composition of solder.

Use the checklist shown to check that you are completing each stage carefully and correctly.

Draw a circle and a vertical line	The vertical line starts in the centre of the circle.	☐
	The vertical line is drawn with a sharp pencil.	☐
Measure the first angle and make a mark	Base line of the protractor is aligned on the vertical line.	☐
	Centre of the protractor is over the centre of the circle.	☐
	Correct scale on the protractor is used.	☐
Draw the radius line from the centre to the mark	Ruler is closely lined up to the centre point and angle mark.	☐
Repeat for the next angle	Repeat checks.	☐
	Final angle is 18°.	☐
Add labels (or shading and a key)	Labels or a key are added.	☐

LOOK OUT

When the angle is greater than 180°, subtract the angle from 360° and measure this new angle anticlockwise.

Maths focus 3: Drawing line graphs

KEY WORDS

best-fit line: a straight line or a smooth curve drawn on a graph that passes through or close to as many of the data points as possible; it represents the best estimate of the relationship between the variables

coordinates: values that determine the position of a data point on a graph, relative to the axes

directly proportional: the relationship between two variables such that when one doubles, the other doubles; the graph of the two variables is a straight line through the origin

intersect: where two lines on a graph meet or cross one another

linear relationship: a relationship between two variables that can be represented on a graph by a straight linea

non-linear relationship: a relationship between two variables that can be represented on a graph by a curved line

origin: the point on a graph at which the value of both variables is zero and where the axes cross

right angle: at 90° to (or perpendicular)

There are two types of line graph:

- a point-to-point line graph

- a **best-fit line** graph.

In a point-to-point line graph, the plotted points are all connected (point to point). In this type of graph, you assume each point that is plotted shows the actual value of the data.

In chemistry, as for other graphs, the independent variable is plotted on the x-axis and the dependent variable is plotted on the y-axis. Readings are taken over a series of time intervals. There is often no **linear relationship** between the independent and dependent variables. The points do not lie in a straight line; they may even appear to go up and down. The lines between plotted points may not be used to read off values between them.

For example, the point-to-point line graph in Figure 3.11 shows levels of NO_x (oxides of nitrogen) in a city, recorded at intervals of 2 hours.

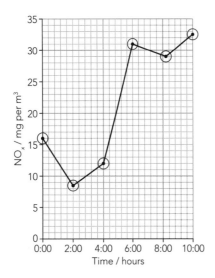

Figure 3.11: A point-to-point line graph showing NO_x levels at different times.

In a best-fit line graph, the relationship between the dependent and independent variables is shown by a best-fit line. A best-fit line may be a straight line or a curved line. It is assumed that the actual values lie on this line (or curve) even if the actual measured values do not, because of measurement errors.

In chemistry, best-fit lines are used to plot data relating to rate of reaction. This is the type of line graph that you will usually need to draw. A line of best fit is also known as a trend line. However, you may see a point-to-point line graph used, for example, to show air pollution measurements at different times in a city in Figure 3.11.

The graph in Figure 3.12 shows how mass varies with volume for aluminium. The graph is drawn as a best-fit line because the measured values do not lie exactly on the line, due to uncertainties in the measurements. The best-fit line is closer to the true values.

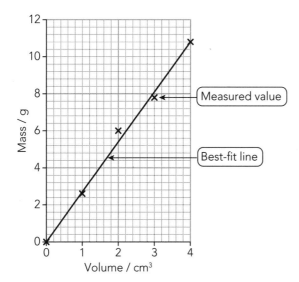

Figure 3.12: The relationship between mass and volume of aluminium.

The graph in Figure 3.13 shows the volume of hydrogen produced every minute during a reaction between magnesium and hydrochloric acid. The points clearly form a curve, but do not lie exactly on the curve. A best-fit curve gives a better indication of the true values.

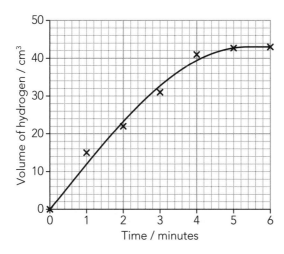

Figure 3.13: The volume of hydrogen produced over time.

What maths skills do you need to draw a line graph?

1	Choosing which variable goes on which axis	• Identify the independent and dependent variables. • Name the variable that goes on each axis.
2	Drawing the axes	• Select an appropriate range and scale for each axis. • Draw the axes and mark the scales. • Label each axis with the correct variable and its units.
3	Plotting the data points	• Find the values of a pair of measurements on the axes. • Find the **intersect** and mark with a dot. • Either draw a small circle around this dot or mark a small cross with the centre exactly over the dot.
4	Using a ruler to draw a best-fit line	• Place a transparent ruler roughly in line with the points. • Adjust the ruler to ensure a best-fit line. • Draw the line carefully.
5	Drawing a best-fit curve freehand	• Visualise the shape of the curve. • Practise drawing the curve. • Draw the curve.

> **LOOK OUT**
>
> You can use **coordinate** notation to describe any point in terms of the values on the axes. The **origin**, where both values are zero, is written as (0, 0).

Maths skills practice

How does drawing a line graph help to interpret experimental data?

A line graph helps to show the *relationship* between the independent variable and the dependent variable.

A straight line of best fit through the **origin** (0, 0) shows that the dependent variable is **directly proportional** to the independent variable (Figure 3.14a).

A curved line of best fit may show that after a certain value of the independent variable, the dependent variable stops increasing. In chemistry, this may be the time at which a reaction stops and no more product is made (Figure 3.14b).

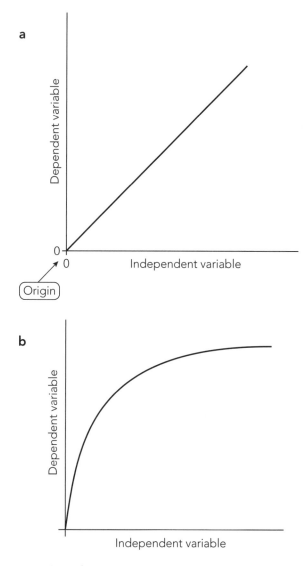

Figure 3.14 a: A straight line of best fit through the origin (0, 0). **b:** A curved line of best fit.

Always think about the chemistry behind the graph. When the reaction between hydrochloric acid and magnesium finishes, no more hydrogen will be produced. The volume of hydrogen will then stay constant, meaning that the line on the graph will become horizontal. The graph must therefore show a curved line of the shape shown in Figure 3.14b. There is **non-linear relationship** between the time and volume of hydrogen produced, so the graph is not a straight line.

See Chapter 4, Maths focus 2 for more information about how lines of best fit can be used in interpreting data.

Maths skill 1: Choosing which variable goes on which axis

WORKED EXAMPLE 3.5

A student has four different samples of aluminium of known volume. She measures the mass of each sample and wants to draw a graph of her results. Which variable should be shown on which axis?

Step 1: Identify the independent variable and the dependent variable.

Key questions to ask yourself:

- Which variable is changed each time during the experiment?

  The volume is changed each time, so volume is the independent variable.

- Which variable is measured each time?

  The mass is measured each time, so mass is the dependent variable.

Step 2: Name the variable that goes on each axis.

The independent variable (volume) goes on the x-axis (horizontal axis).

The dependent variable (mass) goes on the y-axis (vertical axis).

Questions

7   A student measures the volume of hydrogen gas produced every minute during a chemical reaction. He wants to draw a graph of the results.

 a   Name the independent and dependent variables.

   i   Independent variable   ii   Dependent variable ....

 b   i   Which variable should be shown on the x-axis?   ....

   ii   Which variable should be shown on the y-axis?   ....

8   A student reacts hydrochloric acid with sodium thiosulfate and measures the time it takes for the resulting solution to turn cloudy. She then repeats the experiment with different concentrations of hydrochloric acid. She wants to draw a graph of the results.

 a   Name the independent and dependent variables.

   i   Independent variable   ii   Dependent variable ....

b i Which variable should be shown on the *x*-axis? ....

ii Which variable should be shown on the *y*-axis? ....

Maths skill 2: Drawing the axes

WORKED EXAMPLE 3.6

The masses of different volumes of copper are shown in Table 3.11.

Volume / cm³	Mass / g
0	0
1	9
2	21
3	30
4	35

Table 3.11: Masses of different volumes of copper.

Draw suitable axes for a line graph to show these data values. The grid provided is two large squares wide and four large squares in height.

Step 1: Select an appropriate range and scale for each axis.

The *x*-axis needs to fit a range from 0 to $4\,cm^3$. A scale of one large square to represent $2\,cm^3$ fits this range.

As the independent variable was measured every $1\,cm^3$, it is helpful to mark every medium square.

As Table 3.12 shows, a range of $0\,g$ to $40\,g$ would fit on the *y*-axis where each large square represents $10\,g$.

Scale (one large square represents:)	Largest value that can be plotted	Do the data values fit?	Does the scale occupy more than half of the grid?
5 g	20 g	No	Not applicable
10 g	40 g	Yes	Yes

Table 3.12: Table to help work out the scale of the *y*-axis.

Step 2: Draw the axes and mark the scales.

Draw the axes at **right angles** to each other, crossing at the origin. Remember that the axes must be the correct length to fit in the range of data.

Mark the scale with small, neat lines (called 'tick marks') and number the marks.

LOOK OUT

Avoid scales that make the values difficult to plot or difficult to read. Values are easier to read if each large square on the graph paper has a value of 1, 2, 5 or a multiple of a power of 10 of these numbers (10, 20, 50 or 0.1, 0.2, 0.5).

CONTINUED

Step 3: Label each axis with the correct variable and the correct units for the variable.

Write the labels in the form 'variable / units'.

The final axes and labels are shown in Figure 3.15.

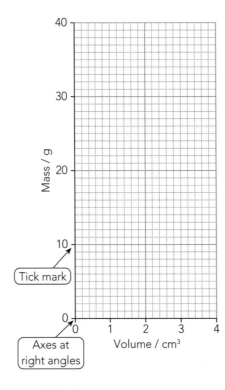

Figure 3.15: The final axes and labels.

Questions

9   The masses of different volumes of caesium are shown in Table 3.13.

Volume / cm³	Mass / g
0	0.0
1	1.9
2	3.8
3	5.7
4	7.6

Table 3.13: Masses of different volumes of caesium.

Draw suitable axes for a line graph to show these data values. The grid is two large squares wide and eight large squares in height.

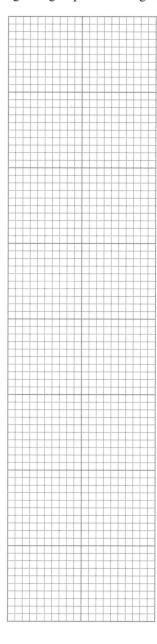

10 The masses of different volumes of lithium are shown in Table 3.14.

Volume / cm³	Mass / g
0	0.0
1	0.6
2	1.0
3	1.6
4	2.2
5	3.0

Table 3.14: Masses of different volumes of lithium.

Draw suitable axes for a line graph to show these data values.

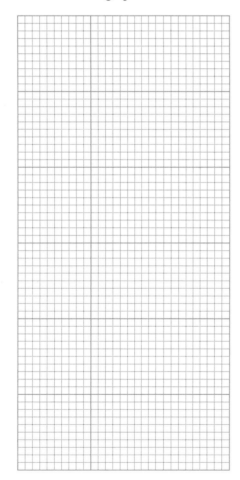

11   Check your partner's axes for questions **9** and **10**. Tick the boxes to show what
they did correctly.

	Q9	Q10
Do the axes occupy more than half the height and width of the grid?	☐	☐
Do the data values fit on the axes?	☐	☐
Do the large squares represent sensible values?	☐	☐

Maths skill 3: Plotting the data points

WORKED EXAMPLE 3.7

The masses of different volumes of copper are shown in Table 3.15.

Volume / cm³	Mass / g
0	0
1	9
2	21
3	30
4	35

Table 3.15: Masses of different volumes of copper.

Plot the data points on a grid with the axes
drawn earlier in Worked example 3.6.

Step 1:   Find the values of a pair of
measurements (**coordinates**)
on the axes.

Find the value of each independent
variable on the x-axis and the
corresponding value of the dependent
variable on the y-axis.

Step 2:   Find the point where they intersect
and mark with a dot.

To do this, track vertically upwards
from the value on the x-axis and track
horizontally across from the value on
the y-axis (Figure 3.16). Mark a small
dot where the tracks meet.

Step 3:   Either draw a small circle around this
dot or mark a small cross with the
centre exactly over the dot.

Repeat for the remaining points.

The final plotted points are shown in Figure 3.16.

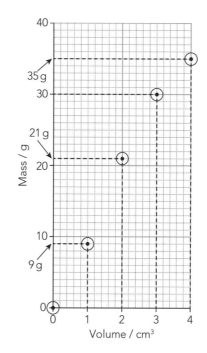

Figure 3.16: The final plotted points.

LOOK OUT

To plot the points
on the graph in the
correct place, you
will need to work
out the value of a
small square. This is
equal to the value
of a large square
divided by 10.

Questions

12 The masses of different volumes of caesium are shown in Table 3.13. Plot the data points on the axes that you drew in question **9**.

13 The masses of different volumes of lithium are shown in Table 3.14. Plot the data points on the axes that you drew in question **10**.

14 Check your partner's graphs in questions **12** and **13**. Tick the boxes to show what they did correctly.

	Q12	Q13
Are the points marked with a dot and a small circle or a cross?	☐	☐
Are the points plotted in the correct place?	☐	☐

Maths skill 4: Using a ruler to draw a best-fit line

WORKED EXAMPLE 3.8

The graph in Figure 3.17 shows the data points for masses of different volumes of copper. Draw a line of best fit for the data points.

Step 1: Place a transparent ruler roughly in line with the data points.

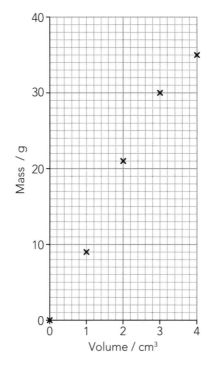

Figure 3.17: Data points for masses of different volumes of copper.

CONTINUED

Step 2: Adjust the ruler to ensure a best-fit line.

Figure 3.18 shows a line with 2 points on the line and 2 points above the line. This is not a best-fit line. Move the position of the ruler until there are roughly the same number of points above and below the line. See Figure 3.19.

Sometimes a point does not fit the pattern. It is an anomalous point. Ignore anomalous points when you draw a line of best fit.

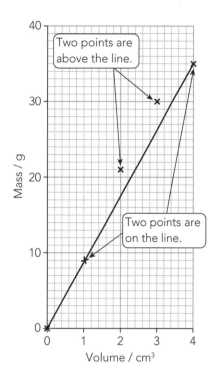

Figure 3.18: This line is not a best-fit line.

Step 3: Draw the line carefully. Always use a sharp pencil.

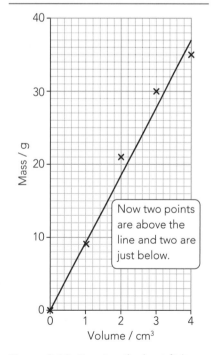

Figure 3.19: Drawing the best-fit line.

LOOK OUT

It is useful to use a transparent ruler when drawing a best-fit line. You can see the relative positions of all of the data points before you draw the line.

Questions

15 a The graph in Figure 3.20a shows the masses of different volumes of lead. Draw a line of best fit.

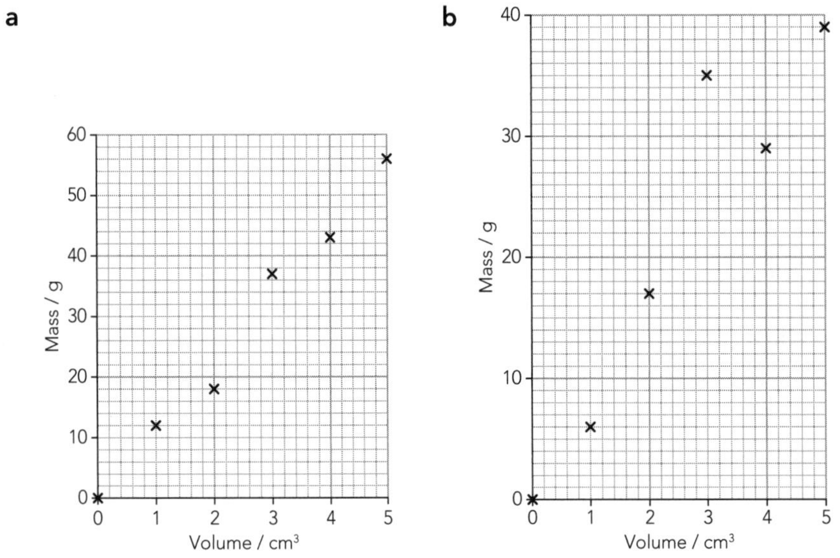

a

b

Figure 3.20 a: Masses of different volumes of lead. **b:** Masses of different volumes of iron.

b The graph in Figure 3.20b shows the masses of different volumes of iron. Draw a line of best fit.

c Compare your lines of best fit with your partner's lines. Are the lines the same? Are there approximately the same number of points above and below each line? Were any anomalous points ignored?

Maths skill 5: Drawing a best-fit curve freehand

Best-fit curves are drawn *freehand*. A freehand drawing is done without using any instruments, such as a ruler or a protractor.

WORKED EXAMPLE 3.9

The graph in Figure 3.21 shows the volume of hydrogen produced each minute when magnesium reacts with hydrochloric acid (HCl). Draw a best-fit curve.

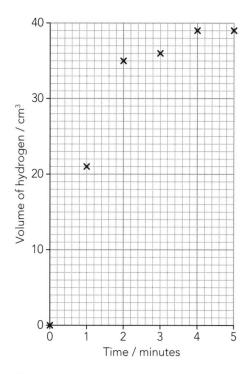

Figure 3.21: Volume of hydrogen produced when magnesium reacts with HCl.

CONTINUED

Step 1: Visualise the shape of the curve.

Look at the graph. Try to picture the shape of the curve formed by the points.

Ignore any anomalous points.

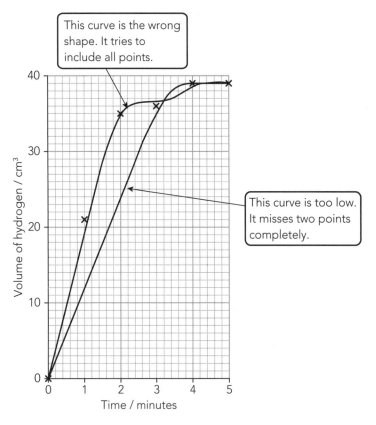

Figure 3.22: Visualise the shape of the curve.

Step 2: Practise drawing the curve.

Using a sweeping movement of the hand (with the wrist or elbow as a pivot), practise drawing a smooth curve without marking the paper.

Make sure the points are distributed roughly evenly on either side of the curve, along its whole length.

Step 3: When you are sure of where you want the curve to go, move your hand with the sweeping movement that you practised and draw the curve. Always use a sharp pencil.

CONTINUED

The final curve is shown in Figure 3.23.

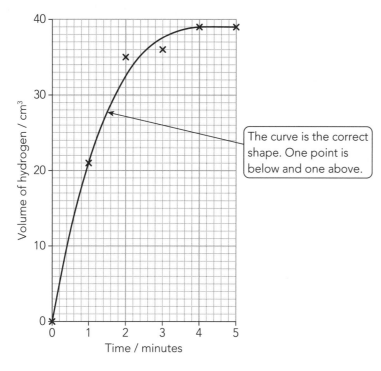

Figure 3.23: The final best-fit curve.

Questions

16 Work in pairs. Draw five dots on a piece of paper. The dots should make a curved shape. Give the piece of paper to your partner.

Ask your partner to draw a smooth curve through all the points. Watch your partner draw the curve. What advice could you give your partner to improve their drawing of the curve?

17 Hydrogen peroxide (H_2O_2) gradually breaks down into water and oxygen. Adding a catalyst speeds up this process of decomposition.

The graph in Figure 3.24 shows the data points for the volume of oxygen produced every 10 seconds when a catalyst is added to hydrogen peroxide. Draw the best-fit curve.

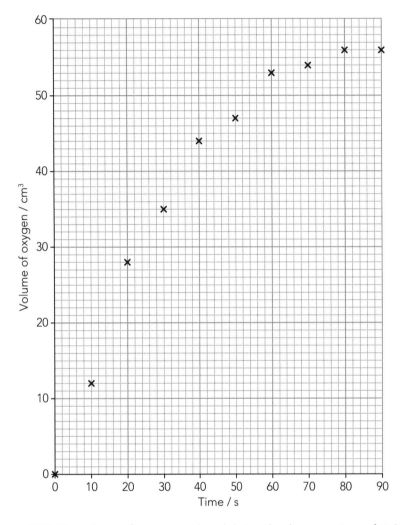

Figure 3.24: The volume of oxygen produced during the decomposition of H_2O_2.

18 A beaker containing hydrochloric acid was placed on a balance and some marble chips were added to the beaker. The mass was recorded every minute. The data points are plotted on the graph in Figure 3.25. Draw the best-fit curve.

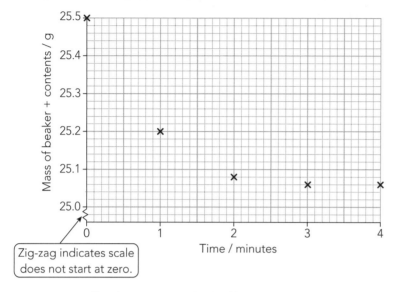

Figure 3.25: Mass of beaker containing hydrochloric acid and marble chips.

EXAM-STYLE QUESTIONS

1 Oxygen (O), sulfur (S), selenium (Se) and tellurium (Te) are in Group VI of the Periodic Table. These elements all make compounds with hydrogen. The melting points and boiling points of these compounds are shown in the table.

Compound	Melting point / °C	Boiling point / °C
H_2O	0	100
H_2S	−85	−61
H_2Se	−66	−41
H_2Te	−49	−2

CONTINUED

a   i   Draw a bar chart comparing the melting points of the hydrogen compounds of the Group VI elements.

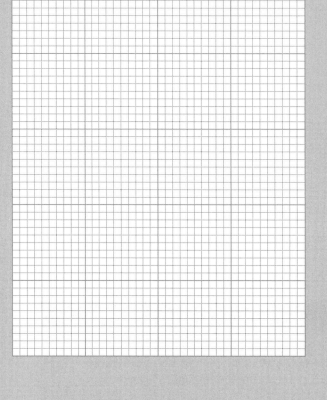

[3]

CONTINUED

ii Draw a bar chart to compare the boiling points of the hydrogen compounds of the Group VI elements.

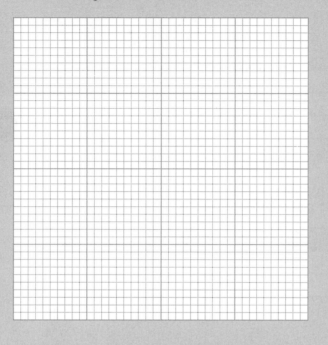

[3]

b   i   One compound does not fit the pattern of melting points and boiling points. State the name of the Group VI element in this compound.

.... [1]

ii If this compound did fit the pattern, what state would the compound be on Earth?

....

.... [1]

[Total: 8]

CONTINUED

2 The percentage of copper in three different types of copper mineral is given in the table. Each mineral is made of a different compound of copper and sulfur.

Mineral	Percentage of copper (rounded to nearest whole number) / %	Percentage of sulfur / %
covellite (CuS)	67	
chalcocite (Cu_2S)	80	
digenite (Cu_9S_5)	78	

a **Calculate** the percentage of sulfur in each mineral. Write your answer in the table. [3]

b i Complete the table to show the angles needed on a pie chart to show the percentage composition of chalcocite.

Element	Angle / °
copper	
sulfur	

[2]

COMMAND WORD

calculate: work out from given facts, figures or information

ii Draw a pie chart to show the percentage composition of the mineral with the greatest percentage of copper.

[3]

CONTINUED

c   Which type of chart is best for comparing the percentage of copper
     in the minerals? Explain your answer.

     ....

     ....

     .... [3]

     [Total: 11]

3   The maximum mass of a salt that dissolves in 100 g of water is called its
     solubility. Solubility changes with temperature. This can be seen clearly
     on a line graph showing the solubility curve.

     a   Draw the axes and plot the points for the solubility curve using the
          experimental data in the table.

Temperature / °C	Solubility of copper sulfate in 100 g water / g
0	14
10	17
20	21
30	30
40	29
50	32
60	42
70	47
80	56

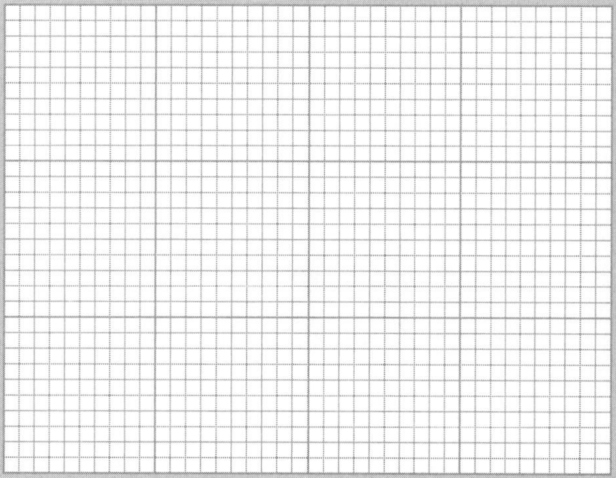

[3]

     b   Circle any anomalous points.   [1]
     c   Draw a line or curve of best fit.   [2]

     [Total: 6]

Chapter 4

> Interpreting data

WHY DO YOU NEED TO INTERPRET DATA IN CHEMISTRY?

- Any experimental data that you collect needs to be interpreted. You need to understand what the data mean.

- A chart or graph shows quantitative data in a visual way.

- Plotting data as a chart or graph makes it easier to discover patterns, trends or relationships between variables.

Maths focus 1: Interpreting charts

Bar charts and pie charts show categories of data, but in different ways.

The heights of the bars on a bar chart show the value of each category.

The bar chart in Figure 4.1 shows the energy produced (per gram) from different types of fuel.

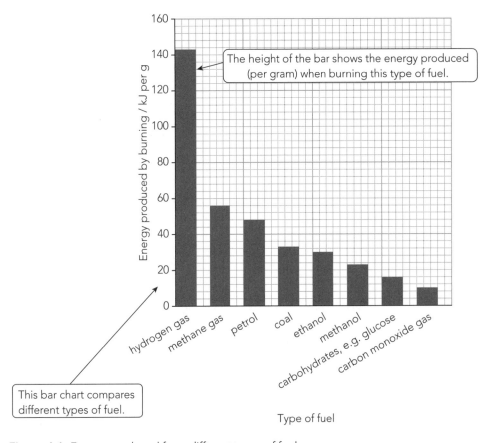

Figure 4.1: Energy produced from different types of fuel.

The sectors on a pie chart allow you to compare the percentages of the whole represented by each category of data.

The pie chart in Figure 4.2 shows the percentages of different elements in a type of dental amalgam.

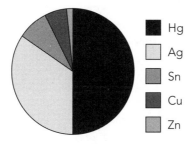

Hg

Ag

Sn

Cu

Zn

Figure 4.2: Percentages of elements in dental amalgam.

What maths skills do you need to interpret charts?

1	Interpreting the heights of bars on a bar chart	• Identify any trends or patterns.
		• Work out the scale on the *y*-axis.
		• Compare the height of the bars numerically.
2	Comparing the sizes of sectors on a pie chart	• Identify the category represented by the largest sector.
		• Estimate the percentage of the larger sectors.
		• Identify the category represented by the smallest sector.

Maths skills practice

How does interpreting charts help you to compare data?

You can use charts to display different types of data. This will help you to compare the data.

You can use a bar chart to compare categories, such as the quantities of different types of material that are recycled.

Bar charts are also useful for showing trends over a period of time. A bar chart can answer a question such as: 'How has the amount of recycling of different types of waste changed over the last 10 years?'

Pie charts can help you to compare percentages and answer questions such as: 'Of all the waste that is recycled, what percentage is made of plastic? What percentage is card?'

LOOK OUT

A trend is shown by a series of data values that change in a certain direction: the data values can increase, decrease or stay the same (e.g. the melting point of Group I (alkali metals) shows a trend to decrease going down the group). A pattern is a series of data values that repeats in a recognisable way (e.g. mean NO_2 levels in a city are highest every morning and evening when people are travelling to and from work).

Maths skill 1: Interpreting the heights of bars on a bar chart

WORKED EXAMPLE 4.1 >

The bar chart in Figure 4.3 shows the percentages of different types of waste that are recycled.

a Identify any trends or patterns.

b Find the highest and lowest percentage recycled.

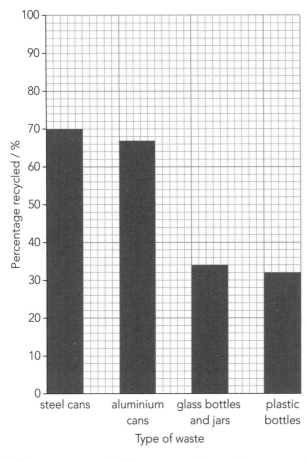

Figure 4.3: The percentage of different types of waste that are recycled.

Step 1: Identify any trends or patterns.

In this bar chart, the two bars for steel cans and aluminium are approximately (nearly but not exactly) equal and show about twice the percentage of glass bottles and jars or plastic bottles. The bar chart does not show a general trend.

LOOK OUT

Trends and patterns are more likely to be found on a bar chart where the categories are periods of time. For example, a bar chart with years as the categories could be used to show changes in pollution levels over a century.

CONTINUED

Step 2: Work out the scale used on the *y*-axis.

One large square represents 20%.

Step 3: Compare the height of the bars numerically.

The category of waste with the highest percentage recycled is shown by the tallest bar (steel cans), and the category of waste with the lowest percentage is shown by the shortest bar (plastic bottles). Track across horizontally from the top of each bar to read the value on the *y*-axis (on the left). The highest percentage recycled is 70% (steel cans). The lowest percentage recycled is 32% (plastic bottles).

> **LOOK OUT**
>
> The percentages in Worked example 4.1 cannot be shown on a pie chart. Think about why this is.

See Chapter 3, Maths Focus 2 for more information about what percentage data may be shown in a pie chart.

Questions

1 Work in a group. Look at the four different bar charts **A** to **D** in Figure 4.4. One person should volunteer to be describer.

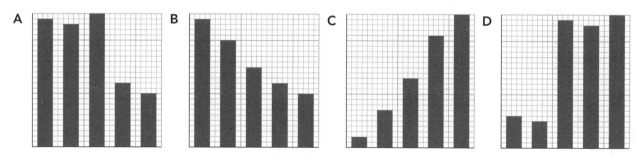

Figure 4.4: Four different bar charts **A** to **D**.

Describer: Choose one of the bar charts **A** to **D**. Describe the trend or pattern shown by the chart to your group. Include words such as:

increase   decrease   gradual   sudden

Group: Identify which bar chart your describer is describing.

Now change describers and repeat the exercise.

2   The bar chart in Figure 4.5 shows the boiling points of the alkanes.

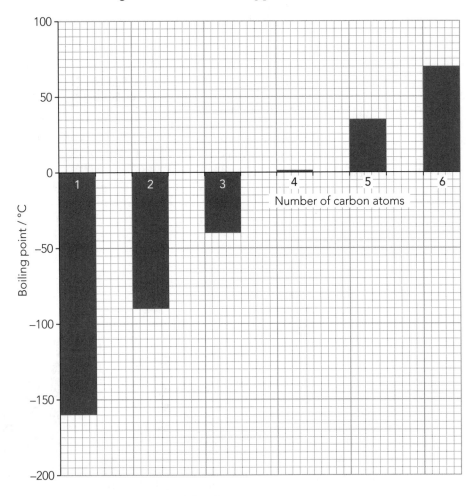

Figure 4.5: The boiling points of the alkanes.

a   Describe any trends shown in the bar chart.

....

....

b   i   Find the boiling point of the alkane with the lowest boiling point
         (to the nearest 5 °C).

         ....

    ii   Find the boiling point of the alkane with the highest boiling point
         (to the nearest 5 °C).

         ....

Maths skill 2: Comparing the sizes of sectors on a pie chart

It helps if you can easily recognise key percentages as fractions of a whole circle (Table 4.1).

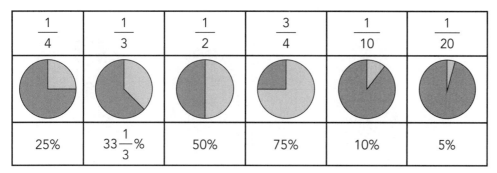

$\dfrac{1}{4}$	$\dfrac{1}{3}$	$\dfrac{1}{2}$	$\dfrac{3}{4}$	$\dfrac{1}{10}$	$\dfrac{1}{20}$
25%	$33\dfrac{1}{3}\%$	50%	75%	10%	5%

Table 4.1: Key percentages of a circle.

WORKED EXAMPLE 4.2

Fertilisers are made up of compounds that provide elements important for plant growth combined with filler ingredients that help disperse the chemicals. The pie chart in Figure 4.6 compares the percentage of each important element provided by a fertiliser.

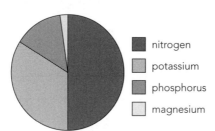

- nitrogen
- potassium
- phosphorus
- magnesium

Figure 4.6: Percentages of elements that support plant growth in a fertiliser.

a Identify the element that has the largest percentage.

b Estimate the percentage of this element and the element with the second largest percentage.

c Identify the element that has the smallest percentage.

Step 1: Identify the category represented by the largest sector.

The largest sector is nitrogen.

Step 2: Estimate the percentages represented by the larger sectors.

The percentage of nitrogen is about 50% (a half).

The percentage of potassium is about 33% (a third).

Step 3: Identify the category represented by the smallest sector.

The smallest sector represents magnesium.

LOOK OUT

If a type of fertiliser only provides nitrogen then 100% of the important elements provided by that fertiliser would be nitrogen.

LOOK OUT

Sometimes the smallest sector in a pie chart represents more than one category, such as 'Others'.

Questions

3   Work in pairs. NPK fertilisers provide different percentages of three elements that are important for plant growth: nitrogen (N), phosphorus (P) and potassium (K). The compositions of four types of NPK fertiliser **A** to **D** are shown in the pie charts in Figure 4.7.

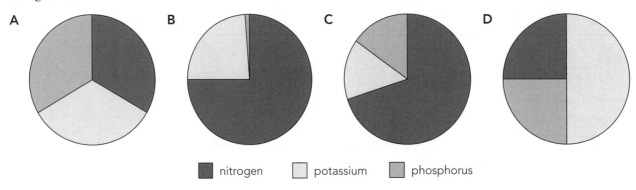

Figure 4.7: Percentages of important elements provided by four types of NPK fertiliser.

For each fertiliser, estimate the fraction and percentage of nitrogen (N), phosphorus (P) and potassium (K). Write your answers in the table.

Fertiliser	Fraction N	Percentage N	Fraction P	Percentage P	Fraction K	Percentage K
A						
B						
C						
D						

4   The pie chart in Figure 4.8 compares the percentages of different elements provided by an NPK fertiliser that also contains sulfur (NPK + S).

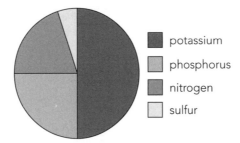

- potassium
- phosphorus
- nitrogen
- sulfur

LOOK OUT

The chemical symbol for the element potassium is K (from the Latin word *kalium*).

Figure 4.8: Percentages of important elements provided by an NPK + S fertiliser.

a   Identify the element that has the largest percentage.

....

b   Estimate the percentage of this element and the percentage of the element with the second largest percentage.

....

Maths focus 2: Reading values from a line graph

KEY WORDS

extrapolate: extending the line of best fit on a graph beyond the range of the data, in order to estimate values not within the data set

intercept: the point at which a line on a graph crosses one of the axes; usually refers to the intercept with the vertical axis

interpolate: on a graph, to estimate the value of a variable from the value of the other variable, using a best-fit line; on a scale, to estimate a measurement that falls between two scale marks

When you draw a line graph, you use a fixed set of data. Once you have drawn the best-fit line or curve, you can work out, or **interpolate**, values between your data points. This interpolation allows you to determine new values *within* the range of the original data.

The graph in Figure 4.9 shows the measured mass of four samples of a bronze alloy with known volumes of $1\,cm^3$, $2\,cm^3$, $3\,cm^3$ and $4\,cm^3$. $0\,cm^3$ of the bronze alloy has a mass of $0\,g$. You can interpolate the graph line to find the mass of bronze with a volume of $1.5\,cm^3$.

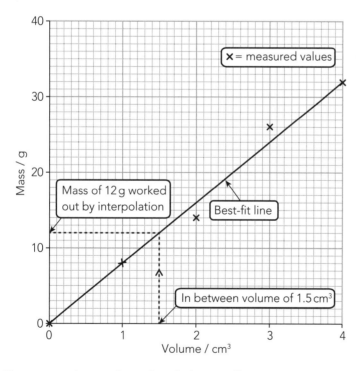

Figure 4.9: The measured mass of samples of a bronze alloy.

Suppose you need to find the mass of $6\,cm^3$ of bronze. You can see that $6\,cm^3$ lies outside the measured range of $1\,cm^3$ to $4\,cm^3$ in Figure 4.9. You can extend or **extrapolate**, the best-fit line and read the value for the mass of $6\,cm^3$. This extrapolation allows you estimate values *beyond* the range of the original data.

You can extrapolate the graph line to estimate values beyond the range of the original data.

You can use extrapolation to find values smaller than the original data and to find where the graph line crosses the y-axis. This is called the **intercept**.

What maths skills do you need to read values from a line graph?

1	Interpolating line graphs	• Start with the known independent value: read up to the best-fit line and then read across to the dependent axis.
		• Start with the known dependent value: read across to the best-fit line and then read down to the independent axis.
2	Extrapolating line graphs	• Place a ruler along the line and draw the extension.
		• Use the extended line to find values beyond those actually measured.
3	Finding the intercept	• Place a ruler along the line and extend the line back until it crosses the y-axis.
		• Read up the y-axis to find the value of the intercept.

Maths skills practice

How does reading values from a graph help you to interpret data about the mass or volume of product at different times?

Data from an experiment investigating the mass or volume of product formed during a reaction often show a non-linear relationship. In a non-linear relationship, the shape of the line graph is not a straight line.

A non-linear relationship makes it more difficult to use maths to find values that have not been directly measured. You can read values from a graph using the best-fit curve.

LOOK OUT

It is often more accurate to read a value from the best-fit line or curve than from a data point that lies above or below the line, because the best-fit line 'smooths out' inaccuracies in the measurements.

Maths skill 1: Interpolating line graphs

Interpolation allows you to determine new values within the range of the original data.

LOOK OUT

If you plan to interpolate a line graph, make sure that you choose suitable scales for the axes. The scales must allow you to read in between values.

> **WORKED EXAMPLE 4.3**

The graph in Figure 4.10 shows the masses of different volumes of lead.

To find a missing value for the independent variable, start with the known dependent variable, read across to the best-fit line, then down to the independent axis.

To find a missing value for the dependent variable, start with the known independent value, read up to the best-fit line, then across to the dependent axis.

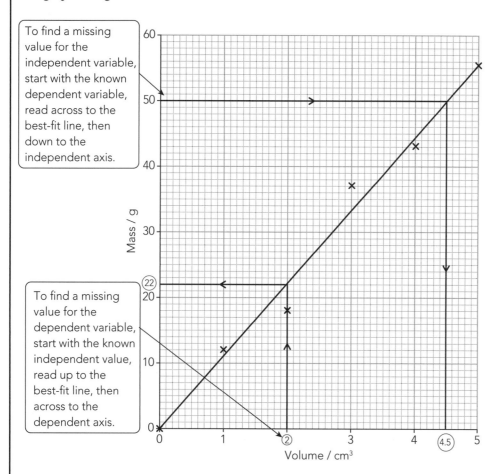

Figure 4.10: The masses of different volumes of lead.

Use the graph to find:

a the mass of 2 cm³ of lead

b the volume of 50 g of lead.

Reading from the graph:

a the mass of 2 cm³ of lead is 22 g

b the volume of 50 g of lead is 4.5 cm³

Questions

5   Magnesium reacts with hydrochloric acid and produces hydrogen gas.
An experiment compared the volume of hydrogen produced by different
masses of magnesium. The results are shown in Figure 4.11.

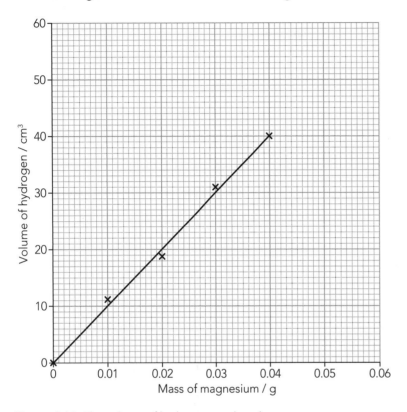

Figure 4.11: The volume of hydrogen produced.

a   Find the volume of hydrogen produced by 0.025 g of magnesium.   ....

b   Write a list of instructions on how to find the volume from the graph.

....

....

....

....

c   Find the mass of magnesium needed to produce 35 cm³ of hydrogen.   ....

d Write a list of instructions on how to find the mass from the graph.

....

....

....

....

6 Figure 4.12 shows the volume of hydrogen produced every minute during a reaction between hydrochloric acid and magnesium.

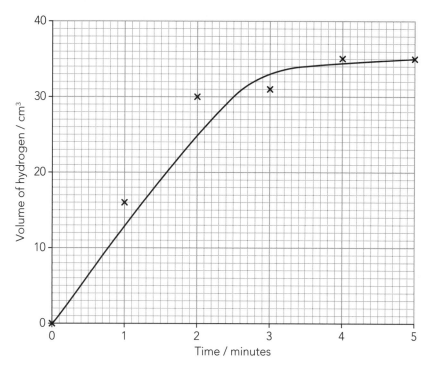

Figure 4.12: The volume of hydrogen produced every minute.

Use the graph to find:

a the volume of hydrogen produced after 0.5 minutes ....

b the volume of hydrogen produced after 1.5 minutes ....

c the time taken to produce 30 cm³ of hydrogen ....

d the time taken to produce 34 cm³ of hydrogen. ....

Maths skill 2: Extrapolating line graphs

Extrapolation allows you to estimate values beyond the range of the original data.

WORKED EXAMPLE 4.4

The graph in Figure 4.13 shows the masses of different volumes of iron.

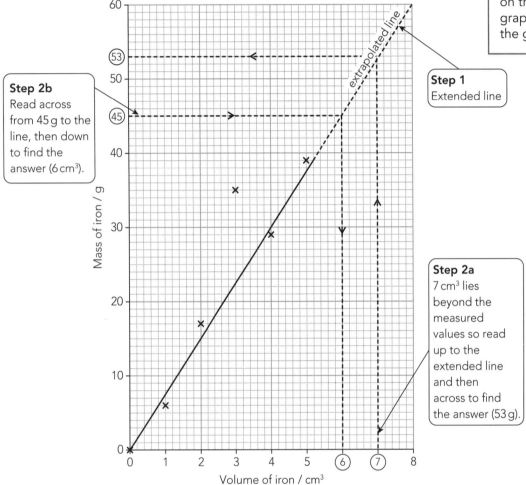

Step 2b
Read across from 45 g to the line, then down to find the answer (6 cm³).

Step 1
Extended line

Step 2a
7 cm³ lies beyond the measured values so read up to the extended line and then across to find the answer (53 g).

Figure 4.13: The masses of different volumes of iron.

a   What is the mass of 7 cm³ of iron?

b   What is the volume of 45 g of iron?

Step 1:   Place a ruler along the line and draw the extension.

CONTINUED

Step 2: Use the extended line to find values beyond those actually measured.

Reading from the extended graph:

a   7 cm³ of iron has a mass of 53g

b   45g of iron has a volume of 6 cm³.

Questions

7   Work in pairs. Look at the graph in Figure 4.14.

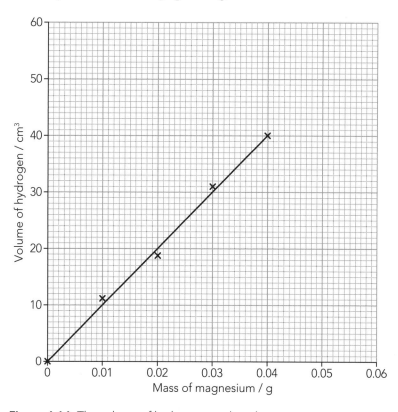

Figure 4.14: The volume of hydrogen produced.

a   Find the mass of magnesium needed to produce 55 cm³ of hydrogen.   ....

Partner 1: Describe to your partner the method you used to find the mass.

Partner 2: Check that your partner has used the correct method.

b   Find the volume of hydrogen produced by 0.045 g of magnesium.   ....

Partner 2: Describe to your partner the method you used to find the volume.

Partner 1: Check that your partner has used the correct method.

8   The graph in Figure 4.15 shows the masses of different volumes of copper.

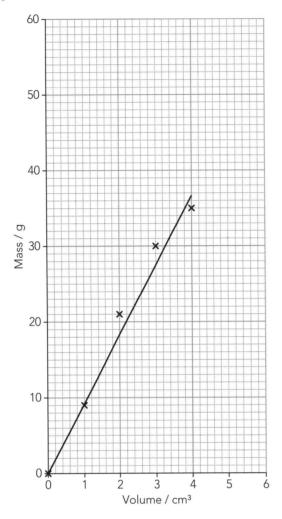

Figure 4.15: The masses of different volumes of copper.

Use the graph to find:

a   the mass of $5 \, cm^3$ of copper   ....

b   the mass of $6 \, cm^3$ of copper   ....

c   the volume of $50 \, g$ of copper.   ....

Maths skill 3: Finding the intercept

The place where the graph line crosses the y-axis is called the intercept. The intercept gives the value of the dependent variable when the independent variable is zero.

Extrapolation also allows you to estimate values of the dependent variable for independent variable values that are less than the range of the original data. Extrapolation can therefore be used to find the intercept (Figure 4.16).

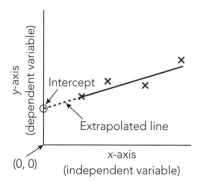

Figure 4.16: Using extrapolation to find the intercept.

WORKED EXAMPLE 4.5

The graph in Figure 4.17 shows the solubility of ammonium chloride at different temperatures. The solubility tells you the mass of ammonium chloride (in g) that will dissolve in 100 g of water. Use the graph to find out the solubility of ammonium chloride at 0 °C.

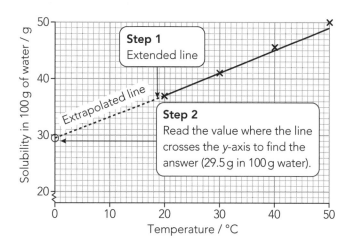

Step 1
Extended line

Step 2
Read the value where the line crosses the y-axis to find the answer (29.5 g in 100 g water).

Figure 4.17: The solubility of ammonium chloride at different temperatures.

Step 1: Place a ruler along the line and extend the line back until it crosses the y-axis.

Step 2: Read up the y-axis to find the value of the intercept.

Reading from where the extended line crosses the y-axis, the solubility of ammonium chloride at 0 °C is 29.5 g in 100 g of water.

> **LOOK OUT**
>
> If the points plotted on a graph do not take up over half of the space, a zig zag may be used to start the values on the y-axis at a number above 0.

Questions

9   The graph in Figure 4.18 shows the solubility of potassium chloride at different temperatures.

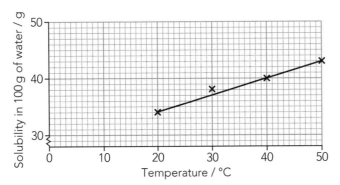

Figure 4.18: The solubility of potassium chloride at different temperatures.

Use the graph to find the solubility of potassium chloride at 0 °C.

....

10 The graph in Figure 4.19 shows the solubility of potassium nitrate at different temperatures.

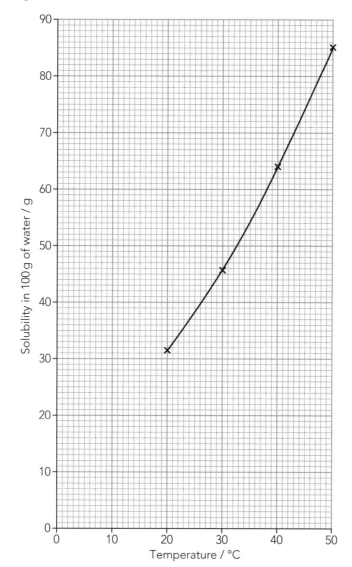

Figure 4.19: The solubility of potassium nitrate at different temperatures.

a   i   Describe how the graph is different to the graph in question **9**.

....

....

ii Decide how you need to change the method to find the intercept.

....

....

b i Use your graph to find the solubility of potassium nitrate at 0 °C.

....

ii Evaluate how accurate this method is compared with the method in question **9**.

....

....

....

Maths focus 3: Interpreting the shape of line graphs

A line graph can give you information without referring to the numbers on the axes. The shape of a graph can show you the relationship between the variables on the *x*-axis (horizontal axis) and the *y*-axis (vertical axis).

The **gradient** (slope) of a line graph can have a scientific meaning, such as the rate of a reaction.

- The gradient of a straight-line graph is constant. To help you think about the gradient of a straight-line graph, imagine you are walking up the straight ramp shown in Figure 4.20. The slope of the ramp remains the same, so the gradient is constant.

Figure 4.20: The gradient of a ramp.

If you need a numerical value for the gradient of a straight-line graph, you can use values from the graph to calculate the gradient.

- The gradient of a curved-line graph changes. To help you think about how the gradient of a curved-line graph changes, imagine you are walking up the hill shown in Figure 4.21. The slope of the hill changes from point **A** to point **C**. The slope at point **A** is steeper than the slope at point **B**, so the gradient at point **A** is greater than the gradient at point **B**. At the top of the hill (point **C**) the ground is flat, so the gradient is zero.

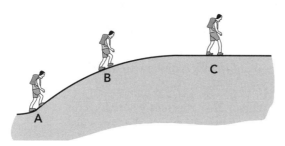

Figure 4.21: The gradient of a hill.

> **LOOK OUT**
>
> A rate of change is a measure of how quickly a variable changes. For example, a rate of reaction could be determined by how much the volume of a gaseous product increases each minute.

Looking at how the gradient changes at different places on a curved-line graph may help you to describe how rate of reaction changes during a chemical reaction.

What maths skills do you need to interpret the shape of line graphs?

1	Recognising the shape of the graph	• Categorise the shape of the graph as showing a linear relationship or a non-linear relationship and as a positive relationship or negative relationship between variables.
		• If the relationship is linear, decide if the relationship is directly proportional.
		• If the relationship is non-linear, state if the graph reaches a maximum or minimum.
2	Interpreting the changing gradient of a curve	• Describe how the gradient changes at different points on a curved-line graph.
		• Link the gradient to a meaning in chemistry.
3	Calculating the gradient of a straight-line graph	• Select two points along the line.
		• Draw a right-angled triangle in which the line between these points forms the **hypotenuse**.
		• Use the triangle to calculate the gradient.
4	Calculating the gradient by drawing a tangent to the curve	• Draw a straight line, touching the curve, that has the same gradient as the curve at that point (the **tangent line**).
		• Select two clear points along the tangent line.
		• Draw a right-angled triangle in which the line between these points forms the hypotenuse.
		• Use the triangle to calculate the gradient.

Maths skills practice

How does the shape of the graph provide you with more information about the relationship between experimental variables?

The shape of a line graph refers to the shape of the line or the curve that is plotted.

Line graphs produced from experimental data show the independent variable on the x-axis and the dependent variable on the y-axis.

See Chapter 2, Maths focus 2, Maths skill 1 for more information on how to identify the independent and dependent variables.

If the line on the graph is sloping *upwards* (as in Figure 4.22a), this tells you that as the value of the variable on the x-axis *increases*, the value of the variable on the y-axis also *increases* (a positive relationship).

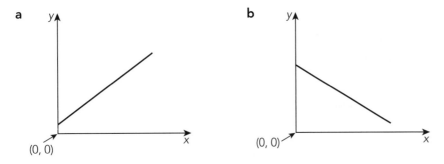

Figure 4.22 a: A positive relationship. **b:** A negative relationship.

If the line slopes *downwards* (as in Figure 4.22b), this tells you that as the variable on the x-axis *increases*, the variable on the y-axis *decreases* (a negative relationship).

If the graph is a straight line, this tells you that the variables have a linear relationship.

If the line passes through the origin $(0, 0)$, this tells you that the variables are **directly proportional**, as in Figure 4.23. This means if a value of the variable on one axis is doubled then the value of the variable on the other axis is also doubled.

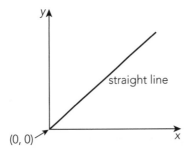

Figure 4.23: A directly proportional graph.

The gradient of any straight-line graph is constant.

If the graph is a curve, you can see that its gradient is continually changing. The relationship between the variables is non-linear.

A curved graph still shows whether the variable on the y-axis is increasing or decreasing when the variable on the x-axis increases.

If the steepness of a curved graph reduces so that the line becomes horizontal, then the variable on the y-axis is no longer increasing or decreasing. This tells you that a maximum (or minimum) value is reached (Figure 4.24).

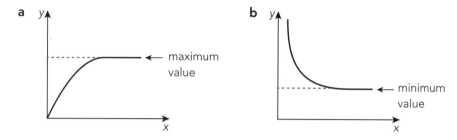

Figure 4.24: Graphs showing a: the maximum and b: the minimum values.

Maths skill 1: Recognising the shape of the graph

WORKED EXAMPLE 4.6

The graph in Figure 4.25 shows how the volume of hydrogen produced in a reaction changes at different times during the reaction.

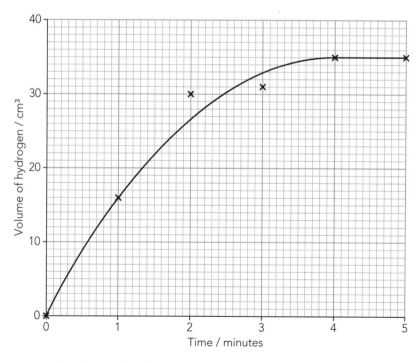

Figure 4.25: The volume of hydrogen produced in a reaction changes over time.

> CONTINUED

Match the graph to the description of the relationship between the variables that it shows. Tick one box to show which is correct.

A   The volume of hydrogen is directly proportional to time.   ☐

B   Volume and time show a negative relationship.   ☐

C   The volume of hydrogen reaches a maximum value.   ☑

Key questions to ask yourself:

- Is the graph a straight line?

  The graph is not a straight line. This means that the relationship is not linear and therefore the variables cannot be directly proportional.

- Does the graph show an increase in the dependent variable as the independent variable increases?

  The graph shows an increase over time. This means that the variables do not show a negative relationship.

- Does the graph become horizontal?

  The line on the graph becomes horizontal. This means that the volume of hydrogen produced reaches a maximum.

Questions

11   Look at each different graph **a** to **c** shown in Figure 4.26. Choose *two* statements from the list in Table 4.2 that correctly describe each graph.

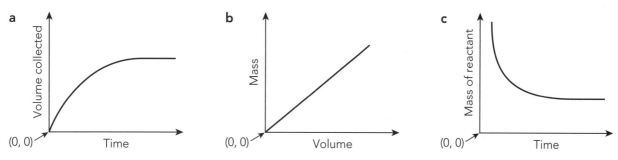

Figure 4.26: Three different graphs **a** to **c**.

Statement A	As the variable on the *x*-axis increases, the variable on the *y*-axis increases.
Statement B	As the variable on the *x*-axis increases, the variable on the *y*-axis decreases.
Statement C	The variables are directly proportional.
Statement D	The graph reaches a maximum value.
Statement E	The graph approaches a minimum value.

Table 4.2: Statements used to describe a graph.

Graph a: Statements .... and ....

Graph b: Statements .... and ....

Graph c: Statements .... and ....

12   Work in pairs.

Partner 1: Draw a freehand sketch of a curved-line graph. Your graph should be based on one of the curves in question **11**. Do not show your partner.

Describe the relationship between the variables on the graph line you have drawn. Try to use words from question **11** as part of your description.

Partner 2: Sketch the graph described by your partner.

Compare your graph to the one sketched by your partner. Do the graphs look similar?

Now change roles and repeat the exercise.

Maths skill 2: Interpreting the changing gradient of a curve

Interpreting the gradient of a curved graph can help to tell the 'story' of a reaction. The gradient of a graph of volume of product (on the *y*-axis) and time (on the *x*-axis) can help to describe how the rate of the reaction changes as the reaction progresses. The rate of reaction at any time during the reaction is equal to the gradient of the graph at any specific time.

WORKED EXAMPLE 4.7

The graph in Figure 4.27 shows the volume of hydrogen produced in the reaction between magnesium and hydrochloric acid. Describe how the graph shows the changes in the rate of reaction as the reaction progresses.

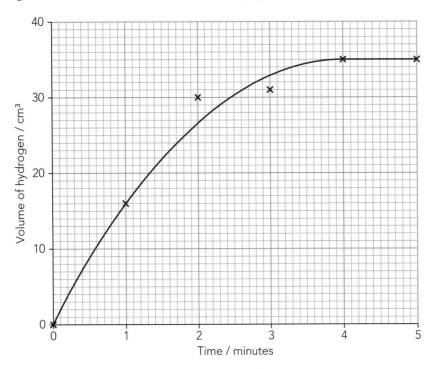

Figure 4.27: The volume of hydrogen produced.

Step 1: Describe how the gradient changes at different points on the graph.

Imagine the curve represents a hill and that you are walking up the hill. Think about where the gradient is steeper and where the gradient is less steep.

The gradient of the graph is greatest at the start of the reaction.

The gradient gradually decreases until about 4 minutes.

Then the graph becomes horizontal. It has zero gradient.

Step 2: Link the gradient to a meaning in chemistry.

If you are asked when a reaction stops, find the point on the graph where the curve becomes horizontal. This is where the gradient, and therefore the rate of reaction, is zero. Then read this time from the scale.

This means that the rate of reaction is fastest at the start and then gradually decreases until the reaction stops by 4 minutes.

Questions

13 The shapes of two hills **A** and **B** are shown in Figure 4.28.

A   B

Figure 4.28: Two hills **A** and **B**.

a   Look at the shape of hill **A**. Imagine that you are walking up and over the hill. Describe the gradient of your walk.

....

....

....

....

b   Look at the shape of hill **B**. Describe the gradient of a walk over this hill.

....

....

....

....

14 The graph in Figure 4.29 shows how the total mass of a flask and its contents changes as a reaction between marble chips and hydrochloric acid progresses.

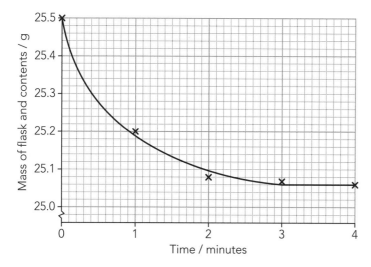

Figure 4.29: The overall mass changes during the reaction between marble chips and hydrochloric acid.

a Describe how the graph shows changes in the rate of reaction.

....

....

....

b Use the graph to determine when the reaction stops.   ....

Maths skill 3: Calculating the gradient of a straight-line graph

The density of a substance is equal to the mass of a sample divided by its volume:

$$density = \frac{mass}{volume}$$

The gradient of a graph is equal to the change in vertical (y) values divided by the change in horizontal (x) values:

$$gradient = \frac{change\ in\ vertical\ (y)\ values}{change\ in\ horizontal\ (x)\ values}$$

The gradient of a graph of mass (y-axis) against volume (x-axis) is equal to the *change in mass* divided by the *change in volume*. This is equal to the density:

$$gradient = \frac{change\ in\ mass}{change\ in\ volume} = density$$

Plotting several experimental values on a graph and drawing a best-fit line should mean that your calculated density is closer to the true value than if you used an individual pair of measurements.

WORKED EXAMPLE 4.8

The graph in Figure 4.30 shows the mass of lead on the *y*-axis and the volume of lead on the *x*-axis.

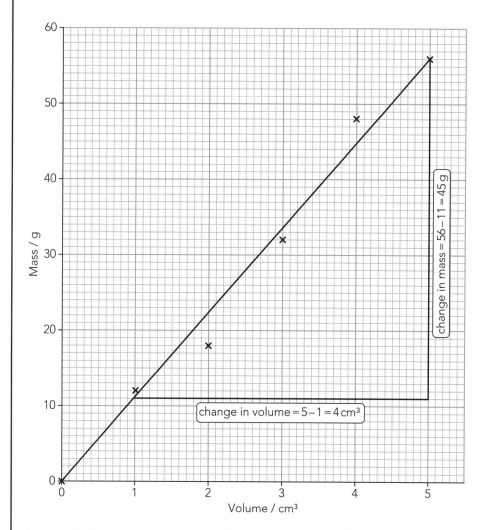

Figure 4.30: The relationship between the mass and volume of lead.

Find the density of lead to two significant figures by calculating the gradient of the best-fit line on this graph.

Step 1:   Select two points along the line.

Ensure that the distance between the points is at least half the length of the full line.

The first point is at $1\,cm^3$ and $11\,g$.

The second point is at $5\,cm^3$ and $56\,g$.

Step 2:   Draw a right-angled triangle in which the line between these points forms the hypotenuse (the side opposite the right angle). See Figure 4.30.

CONTINUED

Step 3:   Use the triangle to calculate the gradient:

$$\text{gradient} = \frac{\text{change in vertical } (y) \text{ values}}{\text{change in horizontal } (x) \text{ values}} = \frac{\text{change in mass}}{\text{change in volume}}$$

$$= \frac{56-11}{5-1} = \frac{45}{4}$$

$$= 11.25$$

Remember to add in the correct units and to round to 2 significant figures.

The units for the gradient should be based on the units for mass divided by the units for volume.

$$11\,g/cm^3$$

This is equal to the density of lead.

See Chapter 1, Maths focus 3, Maths skill 2 for more information about writing numbers to the required number of significant figures.

Questions

15 Calculate the gradient of the best-fit line for the graph in Figure 4.31 to find the density of copper. Record your answer to two significant figures.

....

....

....

....

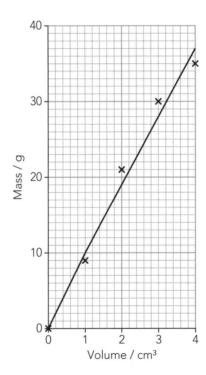

Figure 4.31: The relationship between the mass and volume of copper.

16 Use the graph shown in Figure 4.32 to calculate the density of iron. Record your answer to two significant figures.

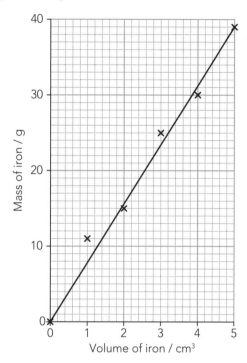

Figure 4.32: The relationship between the mass and volume of iron.

....

....

17 The actual official density values of copper and iron are (to three significant figures):

Copper 8.96 g/cm³   Iron 7.87 g/cm³

How close to these values were your answers to questions **15** and **16**?

....

Maths skill 4: Calculating the gradient by drawing a tangent to the curve

The gradient of the curve of a graph at any point is equal to the rate of reaction at that time.

A tangent line is a line that just touches the curve. The gradient of the tangent line is equal to the gradient of the curve at the point where it touches (Figure 4.33). You can use a tangent line to find the rate of reaction at a specific time during a chemical reaction.

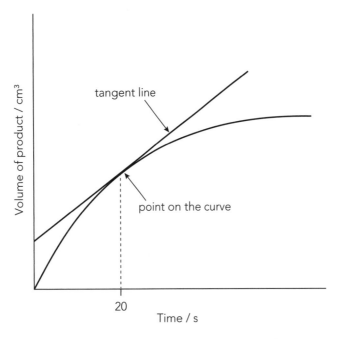

Figure 4.33: The gradient of the tangent line is equal to the rate of reaction at 20 seconds.

WORKED EXAMPLE 4.9

Hydrogen peroxide (H_2O_2) decomposes to form water and oxygen. A catalyst can speed up this reaction. Calculate the rate of reaction at 0 seconds (the start of the reaction) from the graph in Figure 4.34.

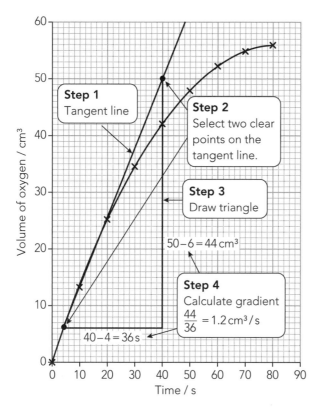

Figure 4.34: The volume of oxygen produced during the decomposition of H_2O_2.

Step 1: Draw a straight line, touching the curve, that has the same gradient as the curve at that point (the tangent line).

Step 2: Select two clear points along the tangent line.

Step 3: Draw a right-angled triangle in which the line between these points forms the hypotenuse.

Step 4: Use the triangle to calculate the gradient.

$$\text{gradient} = \frac{\text{change in vertical } (y) \text{ values}}{\text{change in horizontal } (x) \text{ values}}$$

$$= \frac{(50-6)}{(40-4)} = \frac{44}{36} = 1.2 \, \text{cm}^3/\text{s}$$

Questions

18 For the same reaction, for the graph in Figure 4.35, use a tangent line to calculate the rate of reaction at 50 seconds.

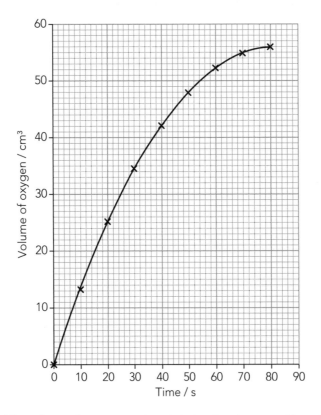

Figure 4.35: The volume of oxygen produced during the decomposition of H_2O_2.

....

....

....

19 Magnesium reacts with hydrochloric acid producing hydrogen gas. The graph in Figure 4.36 shows the volume of hydrogen produced each minute.

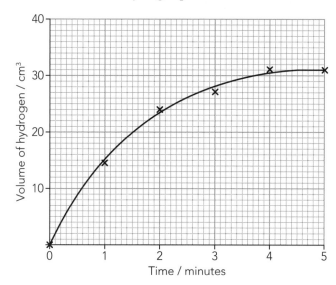

Figure 4.36: The volume of hydrogen produced.

a   Draw a tangent line on the graph that shows the gradient of the curve when the time is 2 minutes.

b   Calculate the gradient of the tangent line to find the rate of reaction at 2 minutes.

....

....

....

c   Work in pairs. Write down the rate of reaction at 5 minutes. Explain to your partner why you do not need to draw a tangent line to work this out.

....

EXAM-STYLE QUESTIONS

1   The bar chart shows the melting points of some Group I (alkali metals) elements: lithium (Li), sodium (Na) and potassium (K).

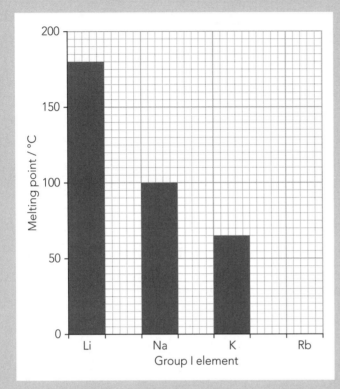

a   i   Find the melting point of lithium to the nearest 5 °C. .... [1]

    ii   **Calculate** the difference in melting points between lithium and potassium.

    .... [1]

b   i   **Describe** the trend shown by the bar chart.

    .... [1]

    ii   Use the trend to estimate the melting point of rubidium (Rb).

    .... [1]

COMMAND WORDS

calculate: work out from given facts, figures or information

describe: state the points of a topic / give characteristics and main features

CONTINUED

c   When lithium and sodium are cut, the exposed surfaces do not stay shiny and grey. They become dull and white through a process called tarnishing. This is because alkali metals react with oxygen in the air to form metal oxides.

i   The pie chart shows the percentage (by mass) of lithium atoms in lithium oxide. Use the pie chart to estimate what this percentage is.

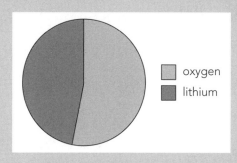

.... [1]

ii   This pie chart shows the percentage (by mass) of sodium atoms in sodium oxide. Use the pie chart to estimate what this percentage is.

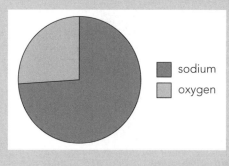

.... [1]

[Total: 6]

CONTINUED

2   The solubility curve shows the maximum mass of sodium nitrate ($NaNO_3$) that dissolves in 100 g of water at different temperatures.

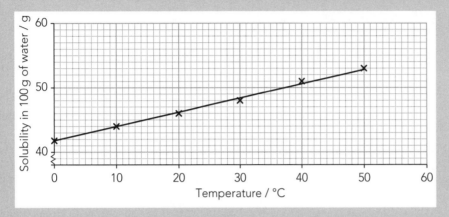

   a   i   Interpolate the curve to find the solubility of $NaNO_3$ at 15 °C.

.... [1]

      ii   Extrapolate the curve to find the solubility of $NaNO_3$ at 60 °C.

.... [2]

   b   50 g of $NaNO_3$ is added to 100 g of water and the mixture is then gradually warmed. Use the curve to find the temperature at which the $NaNO_3$ would be fully dissolved. .... [1]

[Total: 4]

CONTINUED

3 Hydrogen peroxide decomposes to form water and oxygen. A catalyst increases the rate of this reaction. The graph shows the volume of oxygen produced at different times during this reaction.

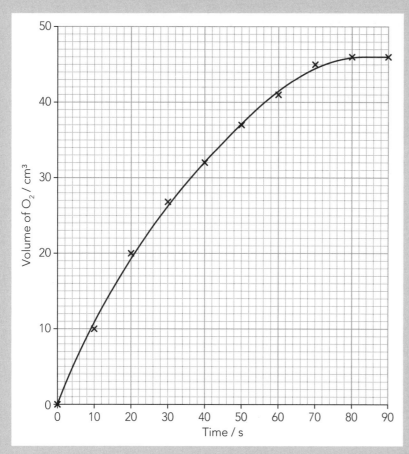

a Describe the relationship between the volume of oxygen produced and time.

....

....

.... [1]

b The gradient of the graph shows the rate of reaction.
   i Use this to work out the units of the rate of reaction.

....

....

.... [1]

CONTINUED

    ii   Describe how the rate of reaction changes during the reaction.

        ....

        ....

        .... **[1]**

c   Use the graph to find:

    i   the volume of oxygen produced after 30 seconds   .... **[1]**

    ii   the final volume of oxygen produced   .... **[1]**

    iii   the time taken for the reaction to finish.   .... **[1]**

    [Total: 6]

Chapter 5

> Doing calculations

WHY DO YOU NEED TO DO CALCULATIONS IN CHEMISTRY?

- Calculations are used in quantitative chemistry to work out numerical information about a reaction.

- For example, you can calculate the mass of a product that will be made from a known quantity of reactants. You can also calculate the mass of reactants needed to make a particular quantity of a product.

- Some calculations are based on the relative amounts of substances reacting and being produced (reacting ratios).

- Other calculations use mathematical formulae that link different physical quantities used in chemistry.

- Sometimes you will need to use data from the Periodic Table in your calculations.

Maths focus 1: Using basic mathematical operations in calculations

KEY WORDS

BIDMAS: 'Brackets, Indices, Division/Multiplication, Addition/Subtraction', which is the order in which mathematical operations are done in a multi-step calculation

operation: a mathematical process, such as addition or multiplication, in which one set of numbers is produced from another

This maths focus explains how to use the four basic mathematical **operations** in calculations in quantitative chemistry. Quantitative chemistry is used to work out numerical answers to questions such as: 'What mass of product will be produced?'

The four basic mathematical operations are:

   addition (+)   subtraction (–)   multiplication (×)   division (÷ or /)

This maths focus also shows you how to do calculations using powers of ten and negative numbers.

To answer a calculation question, you must first use your understanding of the background chemistry to write the correct calculation. Then you must do the calculation in the correct order. This needs an understanding of the maths.

What maths skills do you need to do calculations using basic mathematical operations?

1	Working out the correct calculation for relative formula mass	• Write down the calculation in terms of relative atomic masses. • Find the values needed for the calculation. • Put the values into your calculation.

2	Using mathematical operations in the correct order to calculate relative formula mass	• Use **BIDMAS** to help you remember the correct order of mathematical operations:
		  • complete any calculations in brackets
		  • complete any calculations of indices
		  • complete any multiplication or division
		  • complete any addition or subtraction.

3	Calculating the number of particles using powers of ten	• Write the calculation in full (including powers of ten). • Complete the calculation in the correct order.
4	Using positive and negative values to interpret the overall enthalpy change of a chemical reaction	• Calculate the energy needed to break bonds. • Calculate the energy given out when bonds form. • Calculate the overall enthalpy change. • Use your understanding of chemistry to interpret a positive or negative answer.

Maths skills practice

How does using basic mathematical operations in the correct order help you to calculate different quantities in chemistry?

Using mathematical operations in the correct order helps you to calculate the right value for a range of chemical quantities. Practising these maths skills will help you to calculate:

- relative formula mass (and relative molecular mass)
- number of particles in a given mass of a substance
- overall energy change of a reaction.

Maths skill 1: Working out the correct calculation for relative formula mass

To calculate the relative formula mass (M_r) of a compound, add the relative atomic masses (A_r) of the atoms in one formula unit of the compound.

Before you work on this maths skill, check that you understand chemical formulae correctly.

It is important that you understand what the letters and numbers mean in a chemical formula. The letters show the element symbol for each type of atom that makes up the compound. Each new symbol starts with a capital letter. The small numbers to the right of the symbol (subscripts) tell you how many of that type of atom (ion) there are in each formula unit of the compound (Figure 5.1).

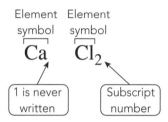

Figure 5.1: The use of subscripts in the chemical formula for calcium chloride ($CaCl_2$).

LOOK OUT

Remember that where there are brackets in a chemical formula, the number of all of the atoms shown inside the brackets is multiplied by the small (subscript) number outside the brackets.

Cover up the right-hand column in Table 5.1 and test yourself. Can you work out the number of atoms (or ions) in each formula unit?

Chemical formula	Atoms (or ions) in each formula unit
HCl	$1 \times H$, $1 \times Cl$
CO_2	$1 \times C$, $2 \times O$
$Mg(OH)_2$	$1 \times Mg$, $2 \times O$, $2 \times H$
$(NH_4)_2SO_4$	$2 \times N$, $8 \times H$, $1 \times S$, $4 \times O$

Table 5.1: Some chemical formulae.

WORKED EXAMPLE 5.1

Write down the calculation that is needed to find the relative formula mass (M_r) of calcium hydroxide. The chemical formula for calcium hydroxide is $Ca(OH)_2$.

Step 1: Write down the calculation in terms of relative atomic masses (A_r).

Remember to use brackets where necessary.

M_r is calculated from A_r.

Use your understanding of the chemical formula of the compound to write the calculation.

M_r of $Ca(OH)_2 = A_r$ of $Ca + (A_r$ of $O + A_r$ of $H) \times 2$

Step 2: Find the values needed for the calculation.

These values may be provided in the questions, but in this case, you need to use the Periodic Table to find the relative atomic masses.

A_r of $Ca = 40$ A_r of $O = 16$ A_r of $H = 1$

Step 3: Put the values into your calculation.

Remember to use brackets if necessary.

M_r of $Ca(OH)_2 = 40 + (16 + 1) \times 2$

> **LOOK OUT**
>
> Relative atomic mass and relative formula mass compare masses and have no units. They give the mass relative to a carbon-12 atom.

Questions

1   **a**   Write down the correct calculation for the relative formula mass of **i** and **ii**.

     i $CaSO_4$ ....

     ii $CaCO_3$ ....

   b   Swap your answers to part **a** with a partner. Check your partner's calculation. Tick the boxes in their workbook to show what they got correct.

     Correct number of each type of atom   ☐

     Correct relative atomic masses   ☐

     Correct mathematical operators used in calculation   ☐

2   Write down the correct calculation for the relative formula mass of **a–e**.

   a HNO_3 ....

   b $MgSO_4$ ....

   c $KMnO_4$ ....

   d $Mg(NO_3)_2$ ....

   e $(NH_4)_2SO_4$ ....

Maths skill 2: Using mathematical operations in the correct order to calculate relative formula mass

Chemical calculations use more than one mathematical operation and often use brackets. It is very important to remember the correct order in which operations and brackets should be performed.

Use the BIDMAS rule to help you remember the correct order to complete the operations in a mathematical calculation:

Brackets, Indices, Division/Multiplication, Addition/Subtraction

WORKED EXAMPLE 5.2

Calculate M_r of $Ca(OH)_2$.

M_r of $Ca(OH)_2 = 40 + (16 + 1) \times 2$ (see Worked example 5.1)

Now follow the rules of BIDMAS.

Step 1: Complete any calculations in brackets.

$$M_r \text{ of } Ca(OH)_2 = 40 + (16 + 1) \times 2$$
$$= 40 + 17 \times 2$$

Step 2: There are no indices in this calculation, so now complete any multiplication or division.

$$= 40 + 34$$

Step 3: Complete any addition or subtraction.

$$= 74$$

Questions

3   a   Use your calculations from question **1** to calculate M_r for **i** and **ii**. Make sure that you carry out the operations in the correct order.

  i $CaSO_4$ ....

  ii $CaCO_3$ ....

   b   Swap your answers to part **a** with a partner. Check your partner's calculation. Did your partner carry out the mathematical operations in the correct order?

4   Use your calculations from question **2** to calculate M_r for **a–e**.

    a HNO_3 ....

    b $MgSO_4$ ....

    c $KMnO_4$ ....

    d $Mg(NO_3)_2$ ....

    e $(NH_4)_2SO_4$ ....

> **LOOK OUT**
>
> Operations must still be used in the correct order inside brackets. Multiplication and division must come before addition and subtraction.

Maths skill 3: Calculating the number of particles using powers of ten

One mole of a substance has a mass equal to its relative formula mass (or relative atomic mass if it is an element). One mole of a substance contains 6.02×10^{23} (Avogadro's constant) atoms, molecules or formula units.

To find the number of these atoms, molecules or formula units, you need to multiply the number of moles of the substance by Avogadro's constant.

Avogadro's constant is a very large number. It is easier to write the number using a power of ten.

See Chapter 1, Maths focus 2 for more information on using powers of ten.

WORKED EXAMPLE 5.3

Calculate the number of magnesium atoms in two moles of magnesium.

Step 1:   Write the calculation in full (including powers of ten).

$$2 \times 6.02 \times 10^{23}$$

Step 2:   Complete the calculation in the correct order. Remember BIDMAS.

Your answer can also be written using powers of ten.

12.04×10^{23} magnesium atoms

If you use a calculator, the answer may be shown in standard form.

1.204×10^{23}

See Chapter 1, Maths focus 3 for more information on standard form.

Questions

5   a   Calculate how many atoms there are in five moles of magnesium.

      i   Calculate the answer on paper.

        ....

        ....

      ii   Calculate the answer on a calculator. Write what is shown on the calculator display.

        ....

  b   Compare your answers to part **a** with a partner. If the answers look different, discuss with your partner why this is.

6   Calculate the number of atoms of copper in the following molar quantities. Write your answers in standard form.

  a   10 moles

     ....

  b   0.1 moles

     ....

  c   100 moles

     ....

  d   0.2 moles

     ....

Maths skill 4: Using positive and negative values to interpret the overall enthalpy change of a chemical reaction

The chemical energy involved in a reaction is also known as the enthalpy (H). Chemical reactions involve a change in enthalpy (ΔH).

The positive (+) and negative (–) signs placed in front of energy values have particular meanings in chemistry.

An energy change in which energy is transferred from the surroundings (taken in by the reaction) is given a positive value. This is an endothermic change and is shown by an up arrow (↑) on an energy profile diagram.

An energy change in which energy is transferred to the surroundings (given out by the reaction) is given a negative value. This is an exothermic change and is shown by a down arrow (↓) on an energy profile diagram.

LOOK OUT

The Greek letter delta Δ is used to represent change.

WORKED EXAMPLE 5.4

Use the data in Table 5.2 to calculate the enthalpy change (ΔH) for the reaction:

hydrogen + chlorine → hydrogen chloride

$H_2 + Cl_2 \rightarrow 2HCl$

Bond	Bond energy / kJ per mol
H–H	436
Cl–Cl	242
H–Cl	431

Table 5.2: Bond energy data.

Step 1: Calculate the energy needed to break bonds.

$$1 \times [H-H] + 1 \times [Cl-Cl] = 436 + 242 = 678 \text{ kJ/mol}$$

Step 2: Calculate the energy given out when bonds form.

$$2 \times [H-Cl] = 2 \times 431 = 862 \text{ kJ/mol}$$

Step 3: Calculate the overall enthalpy change (ΔH).

ΔH = energy needed to break bonds − energy given out when bonds form

$$= 678 - 862 = -184 \text{ kJ/mol}$$

Step 4: Use your understanding of chemistry to interpret a positive or negative answer.

The answer is a negative value. This means that overall the chemical reaction transfers energy to the surroundings. The chemical reaction is exothermic.

Questions

7 **a** The energy profile diagram in Figure 5.2 shows the energy changes when hydrogen reacts with chlorine to make hydrogen chloride.

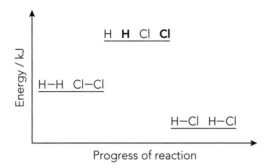

Figure 5.2: Energy profile diagram.

   i   Add an arrow to the diagram to show the energy change when bonds are broken.

   ii Add an arrow to the diagram to show the energy change when bonds are made.

  b Discuss with a partner how the diagram shows that:

   i   the energy change for bond breaking is positive (energy must be put in to break bonds)

   ii the energy change for bond making is negative (energy is given out when bonds are made)

   iii the overall enthalpy change is negative (exothermic).

8 Hydrogen reacts with bromine to make hydrogen bromide.

$H_2 + Br_2 \rightarrow 2HBr$

Bond energy data are given in Table 5.3.

Bond	Bond energy / kJ per mol
H–H	436
Br–Br	193
H–Br	362

Table 5.3: Bond energy data.

  a Calculate the energy transferred from the surroundings when bonds break.

  ....

  b Calculate the energy transferred to the surroundings when new bonds are made.

  ....

c   Calculate the overall energy change for the reaction and state if the reaction is exothermic or endothermic.

....

....

Maths focus 2: Calculating and using percentages

Percentages are often used in everyday life. If you take a classroom test, you may be given your result as a percentage.

'Per cent' means 'out of 100', so a score of 90% means that you got 90 out of 100 ($\frac{90}{100}$) marks.

You can still get a percentage score for a test even if the test does not contain exactly 100 marks. For example, a class does a chemistry test where the maximum mark is 25. To find the percentage score for each student, the teacher divides the student's mark by 25 and then multiplies the fraction by 100 (Table 5.4).

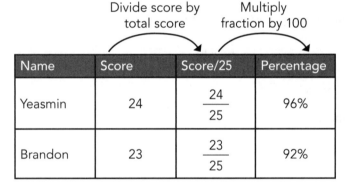

		Divide score by total score	Multiply fraction by 100
Name	Score	Score/25	Percentage
Yeasmin	24	$\frac{24}{25}$	96%
Brandon	23	$\frac{23}{25}$	92%

Table 5.4: How to calculate the percentage from a score.

This maths focus shows you how to calculate and use percentages using chemical quantities.

> ## What maths skills do you need to calculate and use percentages?

1	Calculating percentage composition by mass	•	Write the percentage calculation.
2	Calculating percentage yield	•	Find or calculate the values needed for the percentage calculation.
3	Calculating percentage purity	•	Calculate the percentage, using the operations in the correct order.
4	Using percentages to calculate relative atomic mass	•	Use isotope percentages to calculate the total mass of 100 atoms.
		•	Calculate the average mass of one atom.

Maths skills practice

How does calculating and using percentages help you to find useful values in chemistry?

Percentages have many uses in chemistry. For example, percentages are used to give information about how pure a sample of a metal is. Gold that has a purity of 98% contains 2% of other metals. Percentages are also used to compare the actual mass of product produced with what is theoretically possible (percentage yield).

Practising these maths skills will help you to calculate:

• percentage composition by mass

• percentage yield

• percentage purity.

Maths skill 4 will help you to practise how to calculate relative atomic mass using percentage abundance of isotopes.

Maths skill 1: Calculating percentage composition by mass

A chemical formula shows the relative number of atoms in one formula unit of the element or compound. The formula unit of an element or compound is the molecule or group of ions defined by the chemical formula of the substance. For example, in water (H_2O), for every two hydrogen atoms there is one oxygen atom. In terms of the number of atoms, oxygen makes up a third of the compound.

However, the hydrogen and oxygen atoms have very different relative atomic masses. The relative atomic mass of hydrogen is only 1. The relative atomic mass of oxygen is 16 times greater. The percentage by mass of oxygen in water is very different. It is 89% (to two significant figures).

WORKED EXAMPLE 5.5 ⟩

Calculate the percentage by mass of oxygen in water (H_2O).

Step 1: Write the percentage calculation.

$$\text{percentage by mass of oxygen in water} = \frac{\text{total mass of oxygen}}{M_r \text{ water}} \times 100$$

Step 2: Find or calculate the values needed for the percentage calculation.

To find the percentage mass, you need to know the relative atomic mass (A_r) of each element in the compound.

A_r of H = 1 A_r of O = 16

The chemical formula shows only one O atom, so the total mass of the element is the same as its relative atomic mass (A_r = 16).

To find a percentage, you must always divide by the total amount. This needs to be calculated.

In this case, the total mass of the compound equals the relative formula mass (M_r) of H_2O, which is: $2 \times 1 + 16 = 18$

Step 3: Calculate the percentage, using the mathematical operations in the correct order.

Key questions to ask yourself:

- How can I write out the calculation to make it easier?
  The way you write out the calculation can make it easier to calculate the answer correctly.

  If you write $16 \div 18 \times 100$, you need to remember to use **BIDMAS** and work from left to right.

  You must calculate $16 \div 18$ before multiplying by 100.

  If you write the calculation in the form $\frac{16}{18} \times 100$, it makes it easier to remember to calculate the division first.

  $$\frac{16}{18} \times 100 = 88.88$$

- To how many significant figures should I record the answer?

  Relative atomic mass from your Periodic Table is given to two significant figures, so the percentage by mass should not be written to more than two significant figures.

  This is 89% to two significant figures.

See Chapter 1, Maths focus 3 for more information about significant figures.

LOOK OUT

Make sure you understand the difference between relative atomic mass and atomic number. Always use the correct values in your calculations.

Questions

9 Work in pairs. A student answers the following question.

Calculate the percentage by mass of hydrogen in water (H_2O). Write your answer to two significant figures.

Look at the student's answer.

$$\frac{1}{18} \times 100 = 5.6\%$$

Discuss if the student has answered correctly. If not, find where the student made a mistake in the calculation. Calculate the correct answer.

....

10 For each element, calculate the percentage by mass in calcium carbonate ($CaCO_3$).

a Ca ....

b C ....

c O ....

11 Calculate the percentage by mass. Write your answer to two significant figures.

a N in HNO_3 ....

b Mg in $Mg(NO_3)_2$ ....

c N in $(NH_4)_2SO_4$ ....

....

Maths skill 2: Calculating percentage yield

A chemical reaction does not always produce the yield (mass) of product that is predicted theoretically (by calculation and not by doing the experiment) by the chemical equation. This may be because the reaction is not complete or because material may have been lost when performing the reaction or when transferring and separating the product.

Actual yield is the measured mass of product in a real-life experiment. The actual yield can be compared with the theoretical yield by calculating the percentage yield:

$$\text{percentage yield} = \frac{\text{actual yield}}{\text{theoretical yield}} \times 100$$

A percentage yield of 100% means that the maximum theoretically possible mass of product has been made. A percentage yield of 50% means that only half the mass of product has been made compared with what is theoretically possible.

See Maths focus 5, Maths skill 1, for more information on how to calculate the theoretical yield of a reaction.

WORKED EXAMPLE 5.6

In a laboratory experiment, the reaction between 0.2 g of magnesium and oxygen produced only 0.28 g of magnesium oxide. The theoretical yield of magnesium oxide is 0.33 g. Calculate the percentage yield of magnesium oxide.

Step 1: Write down the percentage calculation.

$$\text{percentage yield} = \frac{\text{actual yield}}{\text{theoretical yield}} \times 100$$

Step 2: Find or calculate the values needed for the percentage calculation.

These values are given in the question.

Theoretical yield of magnesium oxide = 0.33 g

Actual yield of magnesium oxide = 0.28 g

Theoretical yield is used instead of a total. Sometimes you may be required to calculate the theoretical yield.

Step 3: Calculate the percentage, using the mathematical operations in the correct order:

$$\frac{0.28}{0.33} \times 100 = 85\% \ (2 \text{ sf})$$

Questions

12 a A reaction between 0.2 g of magnesium and oxygen produced only 0.22 g of magnesium oxide. The theoretical yield of magnesium oxide is 0.33 g. Calculate the percentage yield of magnesium oxide.

....

....

b Explain why the percentage yield could be less than in Worked example 5.6.

....

13 Copper oxide reacts with carbon to make copper and carbon dioxide.

$$2CuO(s) + C(s) \rightarrow 2Cu(s) + CO_2(g)$$

At the end of a laboratory experiment, 1.2 g of copper was produced.
The theoretical yield is 1.6 g of copper. Calculate the percentage yield of copper.

....

....

Maths skill 3: Calculating percentage purity

A sample of a substance may not always be pure. It may contain small quantities of other substances (impurities). Some situations require a high level of purity, for example, copper used in electrical circuits.

The purity of a sample is given as a percentage:

$$\text{percentage purity} = \frac{\text{mass of pure product}}{\text{mass of impure product}} \times 100$$

LOOK OUT

Percentage purity of a sample is calculated by dividing by the mass of the impure sample.

WORKED EXAMPLE 5.7

An impure sample of sodium chloride has a mass of 5.0 g. The impure sample is purified to produce a pure sample of sodium chloride with a mass of 4.5 g. Calculate the percentage purity of the original sodium chloride sample.

Step 1: Write down the percentage calculation.

$$\text{percentage purity} = \frac{\text{mass of pure product}}{\text{mass of impure product}} \times 100$$

Step 2: Find or calculate the values needed for the percentage calculation.

These values are given in the question.

Mass of pure product = 4.5 g

Mass of impure sample = 5.0 g

Step 3: Calculate the percentage, using the operations in the correct order.

$$\frac{4.5}{5.0} \times 100 = 90\%$$

Questions

14 Work in pairs. A student answers the following question.

A gold ring has a mass of 85 g. The ring contains 22.1 g of other metals. Calculate the purity of the gold.

Look at the student's answer.

$$\frac{22.1}{85} \times 100 = 26\%$$

a   Discuss where the student has made a mistake.

b   Calculate the correct answer.

....

....

15 A silver ring has a mass of 75 g. The ring contains 70 g of silver mixed with small quantities of other metals. Calculate the percentage purity of the silver.

....

....

Maths skill 4: Using percentages to calculate relative atomic mass

Atoms of an element have the same number of protons (and electrons) but can have a different number of neutrons. Atoms with the same number of protons but a different number of neutrons are called isotopes. Some elements occur naturally as different isotopes.

Relative atomic mass is defined as the average mass of naturally occurring atoms of an element on a scale where the carbon-12 atom has a mass of exactly 12 units.

The percentage of an isotope that occurs naturally is called its abundance. You can use the relative masses and abundances of the isotopes of an element to calculate the relative atomic mass of that element.

WORKED EXAMPLE 5.8

Use the isotope data in Table 5.5 to calculate the relative atomic mass of iridium.

Isotope	Abundance / %
iridium-191 (^{191}Ir)	37.3
iridium-193 (^{193}Ir)	62.7

Table 5.5: Isotope abundance for iridium.

Step 1: Use isotope percentages to calculate the total mass of 100 atoms.

$$\text{Total mass of 100 atoms} = 191 \times 37.3 + 193 \times 62.7$$
$$= 19\,225.4$$

Step 2: Calculate the average mass of one atom.

$$\text{Average mass of one atom (and relative atomic mass)} = \frac{19\,225.4}{100} = 192 \ (3 \text{ sf})$$

Questions

16 a Bromine exists as two different isotopes of mass 79 and 81 (Table 5.6).
The relative atomic mass (A_r) of bromine is given on the Periodic Table as 80.

Isotope	Abundance / %
bromine-79 (^{79}Br)	50.69
bromine-81 (^{81}Br)	49.21

Table 5.6: Isotope abundance for bromine.

Discuss with a partner why the A_r of bromine is a value in between the mass of these two isotopes.

b Use the isotope data in Table 5.6 to show that the A_r of bromine is 80 (to two significant figures).

....

....

17 Use the isotope data in Table 5.7 to calculate the A_r of rhenium (to three significant figures).

Isotope	Abundance / %
rhenium-185 (^{185}Re)	37.40
rhenium-187 (^{187}Re)	62.60

Table 5.7: Isotope abundance for rhenium.

....

....

Maths focus 3: Using mathematical formulae in calculations

KEY WORDS

equation: a mathematical statement, using an '=' sign, showing that two expressions are equal; an equation that shows the relationship between variables

rearrange: to manipulate an equation mathematically so that the unknown value can be calculated; also termed 'change the subject'

This maths focus explains how to substitute numerical values into a mathematical formula and how to **rearrange** the **equation** to find other quantities.

The maths focus also helps you to use more than one mathematical formula and the chemical equation to find the concentration of a solution in a titration experiment. Titration is an experimental procedure in quantitative chemistry where a solution of known concentration is used to determine the concentration of an unknown solution.

What maths skills do you need to use mathematical formulae in calculations?

1	Substituting values into a mathematical formula	• List the physical quantities and select the correct mathematical formula to calculate the unknown value. • Write down the values of the known variables and their units. • Substitute the values and units into the mathematical formula and calculate the unknown value.
2	Rearranging a mathematical formula	• Write down the mathematical formula and decide if it is in the form $y = xz$ or $y = \dfrac{z}{x}$. • Identify which physical quantity you are trying to find and rearrange the mathematical formula to put the unknown on the left-hand side of the formula. • Substitute the values and units and calculate the unknown.
3	Using titration results to calculate the concentration of a solution	• Calculate the number of moles in a solution of known concentration. • Use the chemical equation ratio to find the number of moles in the solution with unknown concentration. • Calculate the unknown concentration.

Maths skills practice

How does using a mathematical formula in calculations help you to find out about the amount of a substance?

If you weigh out the relative atomic mass of an element, in grams, it will contain 6.02×10^{23} atoms. This very large number is known as Avogadro's constant and represents 1 mole of the element.

Similarly, the relative formula mass of a compound in grams contains 1 mole of formula units (or molecules). The mass of 1 mole is known as the molar mass and has units of grams per mole (g/mol).

The number of moles, mass and molar mass are connected by a mathematical formula. This makes it possible to calculate the number of moles of a known mass of a substance.

Maths skill 1: Substituting values into a mathematical formula

You need to be able to use three different mathematical formulae.

$$\text{number of moles} = \frac{\text{mass}}{\text{molar mass}}$$

allows you to calculate the number of moles in a given mass of a compound. Make sure the mass is in grams (g) and the molar mass is in grams per mole (g/mol).

$$\text{number of moles} = \frac{\text{volume}}{\text{molar volume}}$$

allows to you calculate the number of moles in a given volume of a gas. Make sure the volume is in cubic decimetres (dm^3).

$$\text{concentration} = \frac{\text{number of moles}}{\text{volume}}$$

allows you to calculate the concentration of a solution. Make sure that the volume is in cubic decimetres (dm^3) and the concentration is in moles/dm^3.

LOOK OUT

It is important to use the correct units. $1\,dm^3 = 1000\,cm^3$, so to convert from cm^3 to dm^3, you need to divide by 1000.

WORKED EXAMPLE 5.9

How many moles of calcium carbonate are there in 0.3 kg of calcium carbonate?

The relative formula mass of calcium carbonate is 100 g.

Step 1: List the physical quantities and select the correct mathematical formula to calculate the unknown. Your list of physical quantities should also include the unknown.

The physical quantities in the question are *mass* in grams and *molar mass* in g/mol. The unknown is the *number of moles*.

Select the correct mathematical formula to calculate the unknown.

$$\text{number of moles} = \frac{\text{mass}}{M_r}$$

CONTINUED

Step 2: Write down the values of the known physical quantities and their units.

Remember to convert any inconsistent units.

Mass has been given as 0.3 kg.

Multiply by 1000 to convert kg to g (300 g).

Step 3: Substitute the values and units into the mathematical formula and calculate the unknown value.

$$\text{number of moles} = \frac{300\,\text{g}}{100\,\text{g/mol}} = 3\,\text{mol}$$

Questions

18 Work in pairs. Three mathematical formulae are often used in chemistry.

A $\quad \text{moles} = \dfrac{\text{mass}}{\text{molar mass}}$

B $\quad \text{moles} = \dfrac{\text{volume}}{\text{molar volume}}$

C $\quad \text{concentration} = \dfrac{\text{number of moles}}{\text{volume}}$

a Identify which formula **A–C** should be used for each calculation in **i–vi**.

    i Calculate the number of moles of carbon dioxide in 2.5 dm³ of carbon dioxide. ....

    ii Calculate the concentration of hydrochloric acid if there are 0.1 moles in 100 cm³ of hydrochloric acid. ....

    iii Calculate the number of moles of magnesium in 5 g of magnesium. ....

    iv Calculate the concentration of sodium hydroxide if there are 0.5 moles in 100 cm³ of sodium hydroxide. ....

    v Calculate the number of moles of carbon in 10 g of carbon. ....

    vi Calculate the number of moles of methane in 4 dm³ of methane. ....

b Now check your partner's answers.

19 Calculate the number of moles of each compound.

    a   10 g of magnesium oxide (MgO)

        ....

        ....

    b   285 g of magnesium chloride ($MgCl_2$)

        ....

        ....

    c   10 g of calcium carbonate ($CaCO_3$)

        ....

        ....

    d   1.8 kg of water (H_2O)

        ....

        ....

20 Calculate the number of moles of each substance in the volume given. The molar gas volume is 24 dm³.

    a   36 dm³ of oxygen

        ....

        ....

    b   3 dm³ of carbon dioxide

        ....

        ....

    c   12 dm³ of nitrogen

        ....

        ....

    d   6000 cm³ of helium

        ....

        ....

LOOK OUT

If you are not given the relative formula mass, remember that you can calculate the relative formula mass from the chemical formula and the relative atomic masses, which you can find in the Periodic Table.

21 Calculate the concentration of each solution.

  a   0.5 moles of hydrogen chloride (HCl) in a final volume of $1\,dm^3$

  ....

  ....

  b   0.5 moles of sodium hydroxide (NaOH) in a final volume of $0.5\,dm^3$

  ....

  ....

  c   1 mole of hydrogen chloride (HCl) in a final volume of $2\,dm^3$

  ....

  ....

  d   0.5 moles of potassium hydroxide (KOH) in a final volume of $500\,cm^3$

  ....

  ....

Maths skill 2: Rearranging a mathematical formula

Mathematical formulae are very useful when calculating the amount of a substance. If you already know the number of moles, you can rearrange the mathematical formulae to find other quantities such as volume or mass. If you know the concentration and volume of a solution, you can rearrange the mathematical formula to calculate the number of moles in that solution.

A mathematical **equation**, such as $y = \dfrac{z}{x}$, shows the relationship between variables.

It allows you to use the values of two or more variables to calculate an unknown variable.

What happens if you know the variable on the left-hand side of the equation, but you do not know one of the variables on the right-hand side of the equation? You need to rearrange the equation so that the variable you want to find is on the left-hand side.

A mathematical equation remains true, provided that the same mathematical action is applied to both sides.

When you are rearranging a mathematical equation, you can use the fact that $\dfrac{x}{x} = 1$

to cancel (remove) some variables. Suppose that the unknown variable was z in

the equation $y = \dfrac{z}{x}$.

Multiplying both sides by x gives $xy = \dfrac{xz}{x}$.

You know $\dfrac{x}{x} = 1$ so the x's on the right-hand side are said to 'cancel,' so $xy = z$.

You can then rearrange the equation by swapping the sides of the equation to give $z = xy$.

You can use the methods in Table 5.8 to rearrange mathematical equations to find any one of the three variables x, y and z.

Mathematical equation	What do you want to find (the unknown variable)?	How to do it
$y = xz$	y	Multiply z by x
$y = xz$	z (one of the two numbers multiplied together)	Swap sides to get $xz = y$ Then divide both sides by x (as it is the other part of xz) to get $z = \dfrac{y}{x}$
$y = \dfrac{z}{x}$	y	Divide z by x
$y = \dfrac{z}{x}$	z	Multiply both sides by x to get $xy = z$ Swap sides to get $z = xy$.
$y = \dfrac{z}{x}$	x	Multiply both sides by x to get $xy = z$ Then divide both sides by y to get $x = \dfrac{z}{y}$

Table 5.8: Methods to rearrange mathematical formulae.

These methods of rearranging will work with all mathematical formula of the same form.

For example, number of moles $= \dfrac{\text{mass}}{\text{molar mass}}$ can be rearranged in the same way as $y = \dfrac{z}{x}$.

> **LOOK OUT**
>
> A *mathematical formula* shows the connection between physical quantities (e.g. density $= \dfrac{\text{mass}}{\text{volume}}$). A *chemical formula* shows the relative numbers of atoms (or ions) in a chemical compound.

> **LOOK OUT**
>
> A *mathematical equation* links different variables using an equals (=) sign (e.g. $y = 2x$). Both sides of the equation are equal. A *chemical equation* includes an arrow ($\rightarrow$) symbol. It describes which reactants are changed into which products.

WORKED EXAMPLE 5.10

Calculate the volume of 0.25 moles of carbon dioxide.

Step 1: Write down the mathematical formula and decide if it is in the form $y = xz$ or $y = \dfrac{z}{x}$.

The formula is:

number of moles $= \dfrac{\text{volume}}{\text{molar volume}}$

This has the form $y = \dfrac{z}{x}$.

CONTINUED

Step 2: Identify which physical quantities you are trying to find and rearrange the mathematical formula to put it on the left-hand side.

The physical property being found is volume.

$$\text{moles} = \frac{\boxed{\text{volume}}}{\text{molar volume}} \qquad y = \frac{\boxed{z}}{x}$$

Multiply both sides by x to get $xy = z$

Swap sides: $z = xy$

$\text{volume} = \text{moles} \times \text{molar volume}$

$\text{molar volume} = 24\,dm^3/mol$

Step 3: Substitute the values and units and calculate the unknown value.

$\text{volume} = 0.25\,\text{moles} \times 24\,dm^3/mol = 6\,dm^3$

Questions

> **Useful mathematical formulae**
>
> $$\text{number of moles} = \frac{\text{mass (g)}}{\text{molar mass } (M_r)} \qquad \text{number of moles} = \frac{\text{volume (dm}^3)}{\text{molar volume (24 dm}^3)}$$
>
> $$\text{concentration} = \frac{\text{number of moles}}{\text{volume (dm}^3)}$$

22 a Look at the questions in part **b**. Discuss with a partner which mathematical formula from the 'Useful mathematical formulae' box you should use for each question. How did you decide?

b Rearrange the appropriate mathematical formulae from the box to calculate:

i the volume of 2 moles of carbon dioxide (molar volume = 24 dm³)

....

ii the mass of 0.5 moles of calcium carbonate ($CaCO_3$)

....

iii the number of moles of sodium hydroxide (NaOH) in 0.25 dm³ of a solution with concentration 0.1 mol/dm³

....

iv the volume of solution with concentration 0.5 mol/dm³ that contains 0.04 moles of sodium hydroxide (NaOH).

....

23 a Given that 36 g of water (H_2O) contains 2 moles of water, show that the M_r of water is 18.

....

....

  b Explain your method to a partner.

  c Use your method to show that the molar gas volume is 24 dm³ given that 2 moles of helium occupy 48 dm³.

....

....

Maths skill 3: Using titration results to calculate the concentration of a solution

To calculate the concentration of a solution in a titration experiment, you will need to rearrange the mathematical formula:

$$\text{concentration} = \frac{\text{number of moles}}{\text{volume}}$$

You can then calculate the number of moles in the solution with the known concentration. The ratio in the chemical equation tells you the number of moles in the solution of unknown concentration. For example, the following chemical equation shows that the ratio of the number of moles of $H_2SO_4 : NaOH$ is 1 : 2.

$$H_2SO_4(aq) + 2NaOH(aq) \rightarrow Na_2SO_4(aq) + 2H_2O(l)$$

Note that (aq) and (l) in the equation are state symbols indicating 'aqueous' and 'liquid'.

You must then use the same rearranged mathematical formula, but with different values, to calculate the concentration of the solution with the unknown concentration.

> **LOOK OUT**
>
> In a balanced chemical equation, the number 1 is not written as part of the balancing.

WORKED EXAMPLE 5.11

A solution of hydrochloric acid (HCl) is titrated against a standard solution of sodium hydroxide (NaOH). It is found that 22.0 cm³ of hydrochloric acid neutralise 25.0 cm³ of 0.20 mol/dm³ sodium hydroxide solution. The chemical equation for the reaction is:

$$HCl(aq) + NaOH(aq) \rightarrow NaCl(aq) + H_2O(l)$$

Calculate the concentration of the hydrochloric acid solution.

Step 1: Calculate the number of moles in the solution of known concentration.

The solution of known concentration is sodium hydroxide.

$$\text{concentration of NaOH} = \frac{\text{number of moles NaOH}}{\text{volume NaOH (dm}^3)}$$

> **LOOK OUT**
>
> To help avoid mistakes, it can help to write the chemical formula of the solution in the mathematical equation:
>
> number of moles (HCl)
> = concentration (HCl)
> × volume (HCl)

CONTINUED

Rearranging the formula gives:

number of moles NaOH = concentration NaOH × volume NaOH

The concentration of sodium hydroxide is given in the question as $0.20 \, mol/dm^3$.

The volume of sodium hydroxide is $25.0 \, cm^3$ or $25/1000 \, dm^3$.

To change dm^3 to cm^3 divide by 1000.

Number of moles of NaOH $= 0.20 \times \dfrac{25}{1000} = 0.005$ moles

Step 2: Use the chemical equation ratio to find the number of moles in the solution with unknown concentration.

$$HCl(aq) + NaOH(aq) \rightarrow NaCl(aq) + H_2O(l)$$

HCl and NaOH react in a 1:1 ratio. This means that every mole of NaOH reacts with 1 mole of HCl.

0.005 moles of NaOH react with 0.005 moles of HCl.

Step 3: Calculate the unknown concentration.

$$\text{concentration of HCl} = \dfrac{\text{number of moles HCl}}{\text{volume HCl (dm}^3)}$$

The concentration of the HCl is unknown. The volume of HCl is the titration volume.

Titration volume $= 22 \, cm^3$ or $\dfrac{22}{1000} \, dm^3$

The number of moles of HCl is the answer to Step 2 (0.005 moles).

$$\text{concentration of HCl} = \dfrac{0.005}{(22/1000)} = 0.227 \, mol/dm^3$$

Questions

24 A titration experiment uses a conical flask to contain $25.0 \, cm^3$ of one solution. The other solution is added from a burette. The volume required to neutralise the solution in the flask can then be measured.

    a $25.0 \, cm^3$ of $0.2 \, mol/dm^3$ sodium hydroxide (NaOH) was neutralised by $21.5 \, cm^3$ of hydrochloric acid (HCl).

        i Name the solution with known concentration. ....

        ii Is this solution in the flask or the burette? ....

        iii What is the volume of this solution? ....

b   25.0 cm³ of sodium hydroxide (NaOH) of unknown concentration was neutralised by 22.0 cm³ of 0.01 mol/dm³ sulfuric acid (H_2SO_4).

    i   Name the solution with known concentration.   ....

    ii   Is this solution in the flask or the burette?   ....

    iii   What is the volume of this solution?   ....

c   Discuss your answers with a partner. Were your answers to parts **a** and **b** different? If so, why?

25 a   The chemical equation for a titration reaction involving sodium hydroxide and hydrochloric acid is:

$$NaOH(aq) + HCl(aq) \rightarrow NaCl(aq) + H_2O(l)$$

Complete the following sentence:

.... mole of NaOH reacts with .... mole of HCl.

b   Complete the following:

    i   0.04 moles of NaOH reacts with .... moles of HCl

    ii   0.16 moles of NaOH reacts with .... moles of HCl

    iii   .... moles of NaOH reacts with 0.2 moles of HCl.

26 a   The chemical equation for a titration reaction involving sodium hydroxide and sulfuric acid is:

$$2NaOH(aq) + H_2SO_4(aq) \rightarrow Na_2SO_4(aq) + 2H_2O(l)$$

Complete the following sentence:

.... moles of NaOH react with .... mole of H_2SO_4.

b   Complete the following sentences:

    i   0.04 moles of NaOH react with .... moles of H_2SO_4

    ii   0.16 moles of NaOH react with .... moles of H_2SO_4

    iii   .... moles of NaOH react with 0.2 moles of H_2SO_4.

27   In an experiment, 25.0 cm³ of 0.2 mol/dm³ NaOH was added to a conical flask. The NaOH solution was neutralised by 21.5 cm³ HCl added from a burette.

a   Calculate the number of moles in the solution of known concentration (NaOH).

....

....

b   Use the chemical equation ratio to find the number of moles in the solution with the unknown concentration.

....

....

    c   **i**   Write down a formula to calculate the concentration of HCl.

          ....

          ii   Which previous answer tells you the number of moles of HCl?

          ....

          iii Is the HCl in the flask or the burette? ....

          iv What volume is used to neutralise the NaOH? ....

    d   Calculate the unknown concentration (HCl).

          ....

          ....

          ....

28 In an experiment, $25.0 \, cm^3$ of NaOH of unknown concentration was neutralised by $22.0 \, cm^3$ of $0.1 \, mol/dm^3$ H_2SO_4.

    a   Calculate the number of moles in the solution of known concentration (H_2SO_4).

          ....

          ....

    b   Use the chemical equation ratio to find the number of moles in the solution with the unknown concentration.

          ....

          ....

          ....

    c   Calculate the unknown concentration (NaOH).

          ....

          ....

          ....

Maths focus 4: Calculating using proportional relationships

KEY WORDS

inversely proportional: the relationship between two variables such that when one doubles, the other halves

This maths focus explains the idea of directly proportional and **inversely proportional** relationships between variables.

You can recognise directly proportional relationships from the shape of a graph (Figure 5.3a). The graph for variables that have an inversely proportional relationship looks very different (Figure 5.3b).

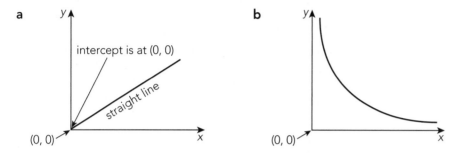

Figure 5.3 a: A directly proportional graph. **b:** An inversely proportional graph.

The graphs have these shapes because of the mathematical relationship between the variables.

If when the independent variable is multiplied by two, the dependent variable also multiplies by two, the relationship is directly proportional. The dependent variable always multiplies by the same number that the independent variable is multiplied by.

If the relationship is inversely proportional, the dependent variable is divided by two when the independent variable is multiplied by two. The dependent variable always divides by the same number that the independent variable is multiplied by.

What maths skills do you need to calculate using proportional relationships?

1	Recognising and using directly and inversely proportional relationships	• Select two values of the independent variable where the second value is two times (or another simple number) the first.
		• Check if the value of the dependent variable for these two values is:
		• multiplied by the same number (direct proportion)
		• divided by the same number (indirect proportion).
		• Use multiplication or division to calculate a missing value of the dependent variable that was not measured.

See Chapter 4, Maths focus 3, Maths Skill 1 for more information on recognising the shape of a graph.

Maths skills practice

How does using proportion in calculations help you to calculate the value for the dependent variable that has not been measured?

If variables are directly proportional, then when the independent variable is multiplied by a number, the dependent variable is also multiplied by that number. For example, the concentration of acid is directly proportional to the rate of reaction. If the concentration is doubled, the rate of reaction also doubles. This means that you can calculate the rate of reaction for concentrations that have not been measured.

For an inversely proportional relationship, you should divide by the number that the independent variable is multiplied by to find the value of the dependent variable.

> **LOOK OUT**
>
> Dividing by 2 is the same as multiplying by ½ (the reciprocal of 2). You can also say that, for an inversely proportional relationship, the dependent variable is multiplied by the reciprocal of the number that the independent variable is multiplied by.

Maths skill 1: Recognising directly and indirectly proportional relationships

WORKED EXAMPLE 5.12

Magnesium reacts with hydrochloric acid to produce hydrogen gas. The data in Table 5.9 shows the volume of hydrogen produced after 1 minute. The reaction was carried out using different concentrations of acid. The same mass of magnesium was used each time. Find the volume of hydrogen produced after 1 minute when the concentration of acid was $0.4\,mol/dm^3$.

Concentration of acid / mol per dm³	Volume of hydrogen produced after 1 minute / cm³
0.1	15
0.2	30
0.3	45
0.4	Not measured

Table 5.9: Volume of hydrogen produced after 1 minute for different concentrations of acid.

Step 1: Select two values of the independent variable where the second value is two times (or another simple number) the first.

The independent variable doubles from 0.1 to $0.2\,mol/dm^3$.

Step 2: Check if the value of the dependent variable for these two values is:

- multiplied by the same number (direct proportion)
- divided by the same number (indirect proportion).

> CONTINUED
>
> The dependent variable changes from 15 to 30 cm^3. It has doubled, so concentration of acid and the volume of hydrogen produced after 1 minute are directly proportional (Table 5.10).
>
> **Step 3:** Use multiplication or division to calculate the value of the dependent variable that was not measured.
>
> Step 1: ×2
>
> | Concentration of acid / mol per dm^3 | Volume of hydrogen produced after 1 minute / cm^3 |
> |---|---|
> | 0.1 | 15 |
> | 0.2 | 30 |
> | 0.3 | 45 |
> | 0.4 | Missing |
>
> Step 2: ×2
>
> Step 3: ×2
> Answer: 60 cm^3
>
> **Table 5.10:** How to use a multiplication factor to calculate an unmeasured value of the dependent variable.

Questions

29 Hydrochloric acid reacts with calcium carbonate to produce carbon dioxide gas. The data in Table 5.11 show the volume of carbon dioxide produced after 1 minute. The reaction was carried out using different concentrations of acid. The same mass of calcium carbonate was used each time.

Concentration of acid / mol per dm^3	Volume of carbon dioxide produced after 1 minute / cm^3
0.1	13
0.2	26
0.3	39
0.4	Not measured

Table 5.11: Volume of carbon dioxide.

a Use Table 5.11 to find the relationship between the variables.

....

....

....

b **i** Calculate the volume of carbon dioxide that was not measured. Write down your calculation.

....

....

ii Write down another way you could have found the same answer.

....

....

iii Sketch the shape of the graph for this data.

> **LOOK OUT**
>
> If you cannot spot a simple multiple between independent variable values, divide the larger number by the smaller number. For example, $\frac{28}{14} = 2$ so $14 \times 2 = 28$.

30 When sodium thiosulfate reacts with hydrochloric acid a solid precipitate is formed. This makes the liquid cloudy. After a time, the cross underneath the flask disappears (Figure 5.4).

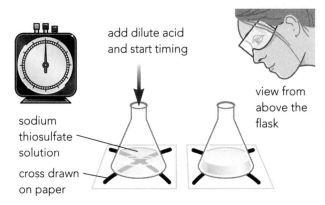

add dilute acid and start timing

view from above the flask

sodium thiosulfate solution

cross drawn on paper

Figure 5.4: Apparatus for the reaction between hydrochloric acid and sodium thiosulfate.

Table 5.12 shows the time taken for the cross to disappear for reactions with different concentrations of sodium thiosulfate.

Concentration of sodium thiosulfate / mol per dm³	Time for cross to disappear / s
0.025	264
0.050	132
0.075	88
0.100	Not measured

Table 5.12: Time for the cross to disappear for reactions with different concentrations of sodium thiosulfate.

a   Use Table 5.12 to find the relationship between the variables.

   ....

   ....

b   i   Calculate the time for the cross to disappear that was not measured. Write down your calculation.

       ....

       ....

   ii   Write down another way you could have found the same answer.

       ....

       ....

Maths focus 5: Calculating using ratios

This maths focus explains the idea of ratio and how ratios are very important in chemistry.

In a chemical formula, the small numbers (subscripts) show the number of atoms of each element in the formula unit of a compound.

- Magnesium oxide (MgO) has a ratio of Mg ions : O ions of 1 : 1.

- Magnesium chloride ($MgCl_2$) has a ratio of Mg ions : Cl ions of 1 : 2.

In chemistry, the word stoichiometry means the ratio of the reactants and products in a chemical equation.

The numbers to the left of each chemical formula in a chemical equation show the ratio of the substances reacting, for example, the balanced chemical equation:

$$2Mg + O_2 \rightarrow 2MgO$$

This shows that magnesium reacts with oxygen molecules in a ratio of 2 : 1.

LOOK OUT

The reacting ratios are correct only if the chemical equation is balanced. A balanced chemical equation has the same number of atoms (or ions) on each side.

What maths skills do you need to calculate using ratios?

1	Using ratio to work out reacting masses	• Use the ratio and relative formula masses to work out the reacting masses. • Calculate the reacting mass required or formed by the given quantity of reactant or product.
2	Using ratio and moles to work out reacting masses	• Calculate the number of moles of reactant (or product) in the question. • Use the ratio to work out the number of moles of product formed (or reactant required). • Convert the number of moles of product (or reactant) into a mass (or volume).

Maths skills practice

How does using a ratio in calculations help you to work out chemical quantities?

A ratio shows the size or quantity, a, of one thing compared to the size or quantity, b, of another thing. It is written in the form $a:b$. In Figure 5.5a, the ratio of carbon atoms to hydrogen atoms is $1:2$ (for every one carbon atom there are two oxygen atoms). In Figure 5.5b, the ratio shown is $3:6$ (for every three carbon atoms there are six hydrogen atoms).

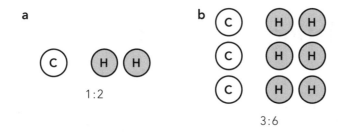

Figure 5.5 a: A ratio of 1 : 2. **b:** A ratio of 3 : 6.

Ratios are usually written in their simplest form using the smallest whole numbers possible. If the numbers on both sides of a ratio are divided by the same number (a common factor), then the ratio is still true.

In this case, dividing both sides of the ratio $3:6$ by 3 gives a ratio of $1:2$ as the simplest form. The ratio of carbon atoms to hydrogen atoms in Figure 5.5b is also $1:2$.

If both sides of a ratio are multiplied by the same number, then the ratio remains true. $1:2$ is the same as $2:4$ (when multiplied by 2) or $3:6$ (when multiplied by 3).

This helps to answer questions such as: 'If the ratio of carbon atoms to hydrogen atoms is $3:6$, how many hydrogen atoms are there if there are seven carbon atoms?'

- First change the ratio into its simplest form $1:2$.

- Then multiply both sides by 7 to give $7:14$.

So there are 14 hydrogen atoms if there are 7 carbon atoms.

Practising these maths skills will help you to use the idea of ratio to:

- calculate the mass of product that can be theoretically made from a given mass of reactant

- calculate the mass of reactant that is needed to make a given mass of product.

Maths skill 2 will help you to practise how to calculate reacting masses (and volumes) using the idea of moles.

Maths skill 1: Using ratio to work out reacting masses

In a balanced chemical equation, the numbers to the left of each chemical formula unit show the ratio in which substances react and are produced. For example, the chemical equation $4Al + 3O_2 \rightarrow 2Al_2O_3$ tells you that 4 aluminium atoms (Al) react with 3 oxygen molecules (O_2). Remember that the number 1 is not written in chemical formulae or chemical equations, for example $2Mg + O_2 \rightarrow 2MgO$.

Using relative atomic mass and relative formula mass, it is possible to work out the mass of product produced by a given mass of reactant. You can also work out the reverse, the mass of reactant required to make a particular mass of product.

In real life, the actual amount of product (the actual yield) may be lower than the calculated amount of product (the theoretical yield).

$$\text{percentage yield} = \frac{\text{actual yield}}{\text{theoretical yield}} \times 100$$

See Maths focus 2, Maths skill 2 for more information about calculating percentage yield.

> ## LOOK OUT
>
> If there are no numbers to the left of a chemical formula, then the number should be 1. For example, the chemical equation $C + O_2 \rightarrow CO_2$ tells you that every atom of carbon (C) reacts with one molecule (O_2) of oxygen.

WORKED EXAMPLE 5.13

Finding the mass of product made by a given mass of reactant

Calculate the mass of carbon dioxide produced by 30 g of carbon.

$$C + O_2 \rightarrow CO_2$$

Step 1: Use the ratio and relative formula masses to work out the reacting masses.

According to the chemical equation, the ratio $C:CO_2$ is $1:1$.

Relative atomic mass of $C = 12$.

Relative formula mass of $CO_2 = 44$.

This means that 12 g of carbon reacts to produce 44 g of carbon dioxide.

CONTINUED

Step 2: Calculate the reacting mass required or formed by the given quantity of reactant or product.

Divide by the relative atomic (or relative formula) mass of the reactant to convert the ratio to the form $1:b$.

$\frac{12}{12}$ g (1 g) of C produces $\frac{44}{12}$ g of CO_2

Multiply both sides by the mass of the reactant in the question.

$\frac{12}{12} \times 30$ g of C produces $\frac{44}{12} \times 30$ g of CO_2

So 30 g of C produces 110 g of CO_2 (3 sf)

WORKED EXAMPLE 5.14

Finding the mass of reactant needed to make a given mass of product

Calculate the mass of carbon needed to produce 22 g of carbon dioxide.

$$C + O_2 \rightarrow CO_2$$

Step 1: Use the ratio and relative formula masses to work out the reacting masses.

According to the chemical equation, the ratio $C:CO_2$ is $1:1$.

Relative atomic mass of $C = 12$.

Relative formula mass of $CO_2 = 44$.

This means that 12 g of carbon reacts to produce 44 g of carbon dioxide.

Step 2: Calculate the reacting mass required or formed by the given quantity of reactant or product.

Divide by the relative atomic (or relative formula) mass of the product to convert the ratio to the form $a:1$.

$\frac{12}{44}$ g of C produces $\frac{44}{44}$ g (1 g) of CO_2

Multiply both sides by the mass of product in the question.

$\frac{12}{44} \times 22$ g of C produces $\frac{44}{44} \times 22$ g of CO_2

So 6 g of C produces 22 g of CO_2.

LOOK OUT

Do not round the answer before the end, as this will change the final answer.

Questions

31 When copper carbonate is heated, it decomposes to form copper oxide and carbon dioxide.

$$CuCO_3 \rightarrow CuO + CO_2$$

a Calculate the relative formula masses of $CuCO_3$, CuO and CO_2.

....

....

....

b **i** Calculate the mass of copper oxide formed from 31 g of $CuCO_3$.

....

....

....

ii Explain to a partner how you used the idea of ratio to calculate your answer.

32 Magnesium reacts with oxygen to form magnesium oxide.

$$2Mg + O_2 \rightarrow 2MgO$$

a Calculate the mass of MgO produced by 0.96 g of Mg.

....

....

....

b Calculate the mass of Mg required to produce 0.2 g of MgO.

....

....

....

....

33 Nitrogen reacts with hydrogen to produce ammonia.

$$N_2 + 3H_2 \rightarrow 2NH_3$$

a Calculate the mass of ammonia produced by 0.7 g of nitrogen.

....

....

....

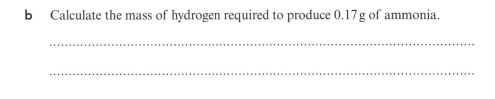

b Calculate the mass of hydrogen required to produce 0.17 g of ammonia.

....

....

....

Maths skill 2: Using ratio and moles to work out reacting masses

You can also calculate reacting masses using the mathematical formula:

$$\text{number of moles} = \frac{\text{mass}}{\text{molar mass}}$$

The mathematical formula:

$$\text{moles} = \frac{\text{volume}}{\text{molar volume}}$$

may be used to find the volume of reactants and products that are in the gas state.

WORKED EXAMPLE 5.15

Finding the mass of product made by a given mass of reactant

a Calculate the mass of carbon dioxide produced by 30 g of carbon.

$$C + O_2 \rightarrow CO_2$$

Step 1: Calculate the number of moles of reactant (or product) in the question.

Use the formula:

$$\text{number of moles} = \frac{\text{mass}}{\text{molar mass}}$$

to work out the number of moles of reactant in the question.

$$\text{number of moles of carbon} = \frac{\text{mass}}{\text{molar mass}} = \frac{30}{12}$$

Step 2: Use the ratio to work out the number of moles of product formed (or reactant required).

The ratio is $1:1$, so $\frac{30}{12}$ moles of carbon dioxide are produced.

Step 3: Convert the number of moles of product (or reactant) into a mass or volume.

To find the mass use the formula:

$$\text{moles} = \frac{\text{mass}}{\text{molar mass}}$$

> **CONTINUED**

Rearranging the formula gives:

mass of CO_2 = number of moles CO_2 × molar mass of CO_2

$$= \frac{30}{12} \times 44 = 110\,g$$

b   Calculate the volume of CO_2 produced.

To find the volume of CO_2 use the formula:

$$moles = \frac{volume}{molar\ volume}$$

Rearranging the mathematical formula gives:

volume of CO_2 = number of moles of CO_2 × molar volume ($24\,dm^3$)

$$= \frac{30}{12} \times 24 = 60\,dm^3$$

> **WORKED EXAMPLE 5.16**

Finding the mass of reactant needed to make a given mass of product

Calculate the mass of carbon needed to produce $22\,g$ of carbon dioxide.

$$C + O_2 \rightarrow CO_2$$

Step 1: Calculate the number of moles of product (or reactant) in the question.

Use the formula:

$$number\ of\ moles = \frac{mass}{molar\ mass}$$

to work out the number of moles of product in the question.

$$number\ of\ moles\ of\ carbon\ dioxide = \frac{mass}{molar\ mass} = \frac{22}{44}$$

Step 2: Use the ratio to work out the number of moles of product formed (or reactant required).

The ratio is $1:1$, so $\frac{22}{44}$ moles of carbon are needed.

Step 3: Convert the number of moles of product (or reactant) into a mass (or volume).

mass of C = number of moles C × relative atomic mass of C

$$= \frac{22}{44} \times 12 = 6\,g$$

Questions

Use moles to calculate your answers to questions **34–36**.

34 When copper carbonate is heated, it decomposes to form copper oxide and carbon dioxide.

$$CuCO_3 \rightarrow CuO + CO_2$$

a Calculate the relative formula masses of $CuCO_3$, CuO and CO_2.

....

....

b **i** Calculate the mass of CuO formed from 372 g of $CuCO_3$.

....

....

....

....

ii Work in pairs. Explain to a partner how you used the ideas of ratio and moles to calculate your answer.

c Calculate the mass of CO_2 formed from 372 g of $CuCO_3$.

....

....

....

35 Sulfur reacts with oxygen to form sulfur dioxide.

$$S + O_2 \rightarrow SO_2$$

a What mass of sulfur dioxide is produced by 3.2 g of sulfur?

....

....

....

....

b What volume of sulfur dioxide is produced by 3.2 g of sulfur?

....

....

....

c What mass of sulfur is required to produce 3.2 g of sulfur dioxide?

....

....

....

36 Nitrogen reacts with hydrogen to produce ammonia.

$$N_2 + 3H_2 \rightarrow 2NH_3$$

a What mass of ammonia is produced by 21 g of nitrogen?

....

....

....

....

b What mass of hydrogen is required to produce 0.34 g of ammonia?

....

....

....

....

EXAM-STYLE QUESTIONS

1 Blue copper sulfate crystals are a hydrated form of copper sulfate. They contain water molecules. White anhydrous copper sulfate contains no water.

a i **Calculate** the relative formula mass of anhydrous copper sulfate with the chemical formula $CuSO_4$.

.... [2]

ii Calculate the relative formula mass of hydrated copper sulfate with the chemical formula $CuSO_4 \cdot 5H_2O$.

.... [2]

b Calculate the percentage by mass of water in hydrated copper sulfate.

.... [2]

[Total: 6]

COMMAND WORD

calculate: work out from given facts, figures or information

CONTINUED

2   Nitrogen fertilisers are made up of compounds containing nitrogen.
    Nitrogen is important for plant growth.

    a   Calculate the percentage by mass of nitrogen in each of these fertilisers.

        i   Ammonium nitrate, NH_4NO_3.

            ....

            ....

            ....   [2]

        ii Ammonium sulfate, $(NH_4)_2SO_4$.

            ....

            ....

            ....   [2]

        iii Urea, $CO(NH_2)_2$.

            ....

            ....

            ....   [2]

    b   Ammonium nitrate is produced by the reaction between ammonia
        and nitric acid.

        $$NH_{3(g)} + HNO_{3(aq)} \rightarrow NH_4NO_{3(aq)}$$

        Calculate the mass of ammonia required to produce 50 kg of
        ammonium nitrate.

        ....

        ....

        ....

        ....   [3]

    c   Calculate the volume of ammonia required.

        ....   [1]

                                                                          [Total: 10]

CONTINUED

3   A blast furnace is used to extract iron from iron oxide.

$$Fe_2O_3(s) + 3CO(g) \rightarrow 2Fe(s) + 3CO_2(g)$$

a   Calculate the number of moles of iron oxide in 16 kg.

[2]

b   i   Use the chemical equation to work out how many moles of iron are produced by 16 kg of iron oxide.

[1]

ii   Calculate the mass of iron produced.

[1]

iii   The actual yield of iron was 10 000 g. Calculate the percentage yield.

[2]

c   During the process, carbon dioxide is produced as a waste product.

i   Calculate the number of moles of carbon dioxide produced by 16 kg of iron oxide.

[1]

ii   Calculate the volume of CO_2 produced (molar volume = 24 dm³).

[2]

[Total: 9]

CONTINUED

4 A student pipettes $25\,cm^3$ of $0.1\,mol/dm^3$ of sodium hydroxide into a flask and adds indicator. The student adds hydrochloric acid from a burette until the indicator changes colour. The student repeats this process three times. The mean volume of hydrochloric acid that the student adds is $15.6\,cm^3$.

The chemical equation for the reaction is:

$$HCl(aq) + NaOH(aq) \rightarrow NaCl(aq) + H_2O(l)$$

a Calculate the number of moles of sodium hydroxide in the flask.

[3]

b Use the chemical equation to work out how many moles of hydrochloric acid the sodium hydroxide reacts with.

[1]

c Calculate the unknown concentration of hydrochloric acid in the burette.

[3]

[Total: 7]

> Chapter 6
> Working with shape

Maths focus 1: Comparing surface area and volume

KEY WORDS

circumference: the distance around a circle

surface area: the total area of the surface of a three-dimensional object

LOOK OUT

Geometry is a section of maths that studies the measurements, properties and relationships of points, lines, angles, surfaces and solids (3D shapes).

A geometric 3D shape has flat surfaces. Each flat surface is called a face. The line where two faces meet is called an edge. Cubes and pyramids are examples of geometric 3D shapes.

The six square faces of the cube in Figure 6.1 are on the outside of the cube. These squares form the surface of the cube.

Figure 6.1: The six square faces of a cube.

LOOK OUT

You cannot see all six faces of a cube on a two-dimensional (2D) drawing. You need to imagine the cube as a 3D solid that you can rotate.

If the cube is cut in half (Figure 6.2), some of the material that was inside the cube is now on the outside surface. This material was hidden but has now been exposed on the cut surface. The **surface area** has increased.

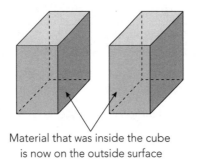

Material that was inside the cube is now on the outside surface

Figure 6.2: A cube cut in half shows how the surface area has increased.

The surface area of a solid is the total area of all of its surfaces. You can calculate the surface area of a mathematically regular shape by adding together the areas of all the individual faces.

The ratio of the surface area to the volume (surface area : volume) is a useful way to compare the total surface area of the pieces of a material with the total volume of the material.

Unlike many ratios in maths, the surface area : volume ratio does have a unit because area and volume have different units. For example, the ratio of $cm^2 : cm^3$ has units of /cm (per centimetre), which is the reciprocal of the distance (cm) used in these measurements.

> **LOOK OUT**
>
> Always remember to include all the faces in your total, even if they cannot be seen in the drawing.

> **LOOK OUT**
>
> It is important that the surface area and volume are given in the same basic unit, for example, cm^2 and cm^3, or m^2 and m^3.

What maths skills do you need to be able to compare surface area and volume?

1	Calculating surface area	<ul><li>For an individual geometric 3D shape:<ul><li>count the number of faces</li><li>calculate the area of each face</li><li>calculate the total area of all of the faces.</li></ul></li><li>If a shape is cut into smaller pieces, find the total surface area of all the pieces.</li></ul>
2	Comparing the surface area to volume ratio	<ul><li>Calculate the total surface area.</li><li>Calculate the total volume.</li><li>Write the full surface area : volume ratio.</li><li>Write the surface area : volume ratio as a single number.</li></ul>

Maths skills practice

How does comparing surface area and volume help you to explain differences in rates of reaction?

Many chemical reactions involve a solid reactant. Only the particles on the outside surface of the solid will come into contact with the other reactant(s). The greater the surface area of the solid reactant, the faster the rate of reaction.

Marble (a rock made of calcium carbonate) reacts with acids. If a block of marble is broken into pieces the mass and volume of marble does not change. A greater surface area of marble is exposed to the acid.

Powdered marble has a higher surface area : volume ratio because the exposed surface area is greater for the powdered marble than for the marble chips, for each unit of volume. Powdered marble reacts with acid more quickly than marble chips because the larger surface area means that more of the powdered marble will be in contact with the acid (Figure 6.3).

> **LOOK OUT**
>
> If you put large marble chips into a beaker it may look as if they have greater volume than the same mass of marble powder. This is because there is air between the marble chips.

Figure 6.3: The rate of reaction of 1 g of powdered marble (left) with hydrochloric acid is much faster than the rate of reaction of 1 g of marble chips (right).

Maths skill 1: Calculating surface area

WORKED EXAMPLE 6.1

Calculate the surface area of a cubic sodium chloride crystal with sides of length 2 mm (Figure 6.4).

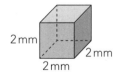

Figure 6.4: A sodium chloride crystal.

> CONTINUED

Step 1: Count the number of faces.

The crystal is a cube. It has six square faces.

Step 2: Calculate the area of each face.

Each face is a square of side 2 mm. The area of each square face is $2 \times 2 = 4 \, mm^2$.

Remember that units of area are squared units.

Step 3: Calculate the total area of all of the faces.

Total area = 6 × area of square face

$= 6 \times 4 = 24 \, mm^2$

See Chapter 1, Maths focus 1 for more information about writing unit symbols.

Questions

1 a Draw a cube. Label the length of an edge. Do not forget to include the units.

   b Calculate the surface area of your cube.

   ....

   c Check that your calculation is correct.

      Tick the boxes to show what you did correctly.

      Is the surface area of one face calculated as length of edge × length of edge or (length of edge)^2? ☐

      Is the total surface area calculated as 6 times the area of one face? ☐

      Are the units used the square of the units of length used in your diagram? ☐

2 Calculate the surface area of a cubic iron sulfide crystal with sides of length 3 mm.

   ....

   ....

3 Calculate the surface area of an octahedral diamond crystal with eight faces (Figure 6.5). Each face has an area of $4\,mm^2$.

Figure 6.5: An octahedral diamond crystal.

....

....

4 A cube-shaped block of aluminium measures $1\,cm \times 1\,cm \times 1\,cm$.

a Calculate the surface area of the block.

....

....

b The block is then cut into eight equally sized cubes each measuring $0.5\,cm \times 0.5\,cm \times 0.5\,cm$ (Figure 6.6).

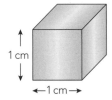 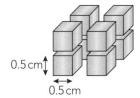

Figure 6.6: A cube-shaped block of aluminium cut into eight equally sized cubes.

Calculate the new surface area of the eight individual cubes.

....

....

....

5 Work in pairs. Figure 6.7 shows a cylinder-shaped container.

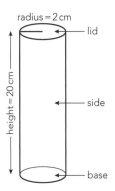

Figure 6.7: A cylinder-shaped container.

The container is made up of three shapes. The lid and base are both circles. The side is a rectangle (Figure 6.8).

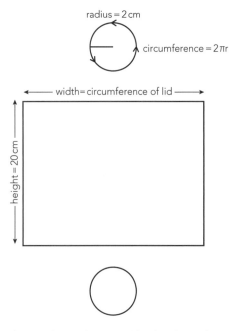

Figure 6.8: The three shapes that make up a cylinder-shaped container.

a Discuss with your partner why the width of the side is equal to the **circumference** of the circular lid. Think about how the side of the cylinder forms a rectangle when it is 'unrolled'.

b Calculate the area of the side of the container.

....

....

c Calculate the total area of the lid and base.

....

> **LOOK OUT**
>
> The circumference is the length of the perimeter of a circle (the distance around the circle) and is equal to $2\pi r$, where r is the radius of the circle.

> **LOOK OUT**
>
> To calculate the area of the circular face use πr^2, where r is the radius. The value of π may be found by using the key on a calculator.

d   Calculate the total surface area.

....

6   Calculate the surface area of a cylinder of chalk with diameter 0.5 cm and length 10 cm (Figure 6.9).

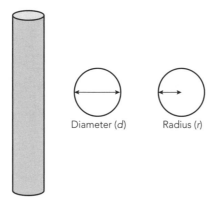

Diameter (*d*)   Radius (*r*)

Figure 6.9: A cylinder of chalk. Note that the radius of a circle is equal to half the diameter.

....

....

....

....

....

Maths skill 2: Comparing the surface area to volume ratio

WORKED EXAMPLE 6.2

Compare the surface area : volume ratio of a 2 cm × 2 cm × 2 cm cube with the surface area : volume ratio when the cube is cut into eight 1 cm × 1 cm × 1 cm cubes (Figure 6.10).

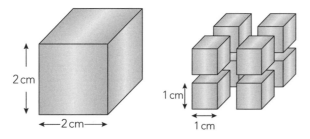

2 cm

←—2 cm—→

1 cm

1 cm

Figure 6.10: A 2 cm × 2 cm × 2 cm cube cut into eight 1 cm × 1 cm × 1 cm cubes.

CONTINUED

The 2 cm × 2 cm × 2 cm cube:

Step 1: Calculate the surface area.

$$\text{surface area} = 6 \times 2 \times 2 = 24 \, cm^2$$

Step 2: Calculate the volume.

The volume of a cube is equal to its length cubed.

$$\text{volume} = 2^3 = 8 \, cm^3$$

Step 3: Write the full surface area : volume ratio.

$$24 : 8$$

Step 4: Write the surface area : volume ratio as a single number with a unit.

$$\frac{24 \, cm^2}{8 \, cm^3} = 3/cm$$

The eight 1 cm × 1 cm × 1 cm cubes:

Step 1: Calculate the total surface area.

$$\text{Total surface area} = 8 \times 6 \times 1 = 48 \, cm^2$$

Step 2: Calculate the total volume.

$$\text{Total volume} = 8 \times 1^3 = 8 \, cm^3$$

Step 3: Write the full surface area : volume ratio.

$$48 : 8$$

Step 4: Write the surface area : volume ratio as a single number with a unit.

$$\frac{48 \, cm^2}{8 \, cm^3} = 6/cm$$

Cutting the cube has increased the surface area : volume ratio from 3/cm to 6/cm.

LOOK OUT

The units of area are squared units (cm^2) and the units of volume are cubed units (cm^3).

LOOK OUT

The basic unit for the volume should be the same as for the surface area to make the ratio valid. For example, if surface area is in m^2 then the volume should be in m^3.

Questions

7   Work in pairs.

a   Discuss with your partner how the surface area : volume ratio of a
3 cm × 3 cm × 3 cm cube (Figure 6.11) compares with the total surface
area : volume ratio when the cube is cut into separate 1 cm × 1 cm × 1 cm cubes.

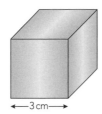

Figure 6.11: A 3 cm × 3 cm × 3 cm cube.

b   **i**   Calculate the surface area : volume ratio of the 3 cm × 3 cm × 3 cm cube.

....

....

....

....

ii   Calculate the total surface area : volume ratio when the cube has been cut
into separate 1 cm × 1 cm × 1 cm cubes (Figure 6.12).

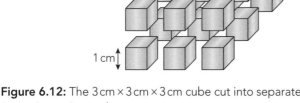

Figure 6.12: The 3 cm × 3 cm × 3 cm cube cut into separate
1 cm × 1 cm × 1 cm cubes.

....

....

....

....

c   Were your discussions in part **a** correct? How does thinking about the answer
before doing the calculations help?

8 **a** Work out the surface area : volume ratio of:

    i one $4\,cm \times 4\,cm \times 4\,cm$ cube

....

....

....

....

....

    ii eight $2\,cm \times 2\,cm \times 2\,cm$ cubes

....

....

....

....

....

    iii sixty-four $1\,cm \times 1\,cm \times 1\,cm$ cubes.

....

....

....

....

....

b Explain why the surface area : volume ratio increases when the $4\,cm \times 4\,cm \times 4\,cm$ cube is broken first into eight $2\,cm \times 2\,cm \times 2\,cm$ cubes and then sixty-four $1\,cm \times 1\,cm \times 1\,cm$ cubes.

....

....

EXAM-STYLE QUESTIONS

1   A student places a stick of chalk into a beaker and carefully pours dilute hydrochloric acid into the beaker until the chalk is completely covered. She then breaks a second stick of chalk into four equal-sized pieces, places the four pieces in a new beaker and adds the same volume of acid. Each stick of chalk was 8 cm long with a diameter of 0.5 cm.

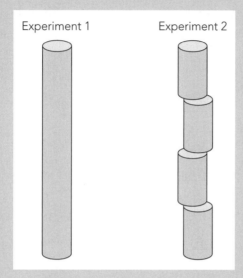

Experiment 1   Experiment 2

a   Circle the factor that the student changed that will affect the rate of reaction?

   A   temperature   B   surface area   C   volume   D   mass   [1]

b   **Calculate** the surface area of the unbroken stick of chalk.

   ....

   ....

   ....

   .... [3]

c   Calculate the total surface area of the broken chalk.

   ....

   ....

   ....

   .... [4]

COMMAND WORD

calculate: work out from given facts, figures or information

CONTINUED

   d **Explain** why the reaction with the broken chalk is slightly faster than with the unbroken stick of chalk.

....

....

....

.... [3]

[Total: 11]

2 Catalysts are used to increase the rate of reaction. In order to work, the catalyst must be in contact with the reactant. Some catalysts are coated onto another surface (e.g. in a catalytic converter used to remove harmful emissions for vehicle exhaust gases). The greater the surface area available, the more reactant can come into contact with the catalyst and the faster the reaction can occur.

Some catalyst support blocks are filled with hexagonal tubes. If the block contained no hexagonal tubes, the catalyst would need to coat the inside faces of one large rectangular block. Instead, the catalyst coats the inside of each hexagonal tube in the structure. Gases pass through these hexagonal tubes allowing the catalyst to catalyse any reactions.

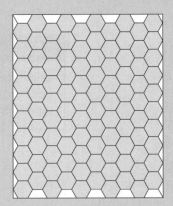
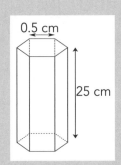

Each hexagonal tube has sides of length 0.5 cm, and the length of the tube is 25 cm.

  a Calculate the surface area inside one hexagonal tube.

....

.... [2]

  b The block contains 100 hexagonal tubes. Calculate the total surface area inside the block.

....

.... [1]

CONTINUED

c   The top of the block is a 10 cm × 10 cm square. Calculate the volume of the block.

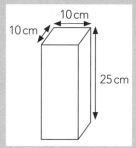

....

.... [1]

d   Calculate the surface area : volume ratio of the block.

....

.... [1]

e   i   Calculate the surface area inside an empty block of 10 cm × 10 cm × 25 cm.

....

.... [1]

     ii   Calculate the surface area : volume ratio of an empty block of 10 cm × 10 cm × 25 cm.

....

....

.... [1]

f   **Compare** the surface area : volume ratio of the empty block to the block containing hexagonal tubes.

....

.... [1]

[Total: 8]

COMMAND WORD

compare: identify / comment on similarities and/or differences

> Applying more than one skill

1 Marble is made of the compound calcium carbonate. It reacts with hydrochloric acid producing carbon dioxide gas.

calcium carbonate + hydrochloric acid → calcium chloride + water + carbon dioxide

$$CaCO_3(s) + 2HCl(aq) \rightarrow CaCl_2(aq) + H_2O(l) + CO_2(g)$$

a Use the relative atomic masses listed in the table to calculate the relative formula mass of:

   i calcium carbonate

   .... **[1]**

   ii carbon dioxide.

   .... **[1]**

Element	Relative atomic mass
Ca	40
C	12
O	16

b Calculate how many grams of carbon dioxide will be produced with these starting quantities of calcium carbonate:

   i 100 g

   .... **[1]**

   ii 10 g

   .... **[1]**

   iii 5 g.

   .... **[1]**

c A student measures the total mass of some marble chips and a flask containing hydrochloric acid. She then adds the marble chips to the flask and measures the total mass every minute. The mass gradually decreases as carbon dioxide gas is released.

Calculate the loss of mass after each minute of the reaction. Record your answers in the table.

Loss of mass at a given time = mass at the start − mass at that time

Time	Total mass / g	Loss of mass / g
0	79.4	
1	78.9	
2	78.3	
3	78.2	
4	77.7	
5	77.5	
6	77.5	

[7]

d   Use the axes to plot a graph to show the loss of mass over time.

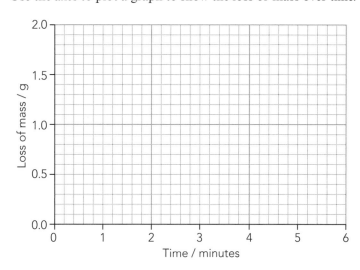

[3]

e   Look at the shape of the graph.

  i   Give the name of the feature of the graph that shows the rate of reaction.

  .... [1]

  ii   Describe how the rate of reaction changes.

  ....

  ....

  .... [1]

  iii   Use the graph to determine approximately when the reaction stopped.

  ....

  ....

  .... [1]

[Total: 18]

2   Vinegar is a solution of ethanoic acid in water. A student carried out an experiment to find the concentration of ethanoic acid in a sample from a bottle of vinegar. First, the student added $25.0\,cm^3$ of vinegar to a conical flask and added a few drops of indicator. Next, she gradually added sodium hydroxide from a burette to the flask until the vinegar was exactly neutralised. She then carried out the experiment two more times.

a   Use the burette diagrams to determine the volumes of sodium hydroxide added from the burette. Record the volumes in the table.

Experiment	Burette diagram	Volume of sodium hydroxide added / cm^3
1	22 — 23	
2	22 — 23	
3	22 — 23	

[3]

b   Calculate the mean volume of sodium hydroxide added.

.... [2]

c   The concentration of the sodium hydroxide was known to be $1\,mol/dm^3$.

i   Rearrange the formula so that 'moles' is on the left-hand side.

$$\text{concentration} = \frac{\text{moles}}{\text{volume (dm}^3)}$$

moles = ... [1]

ii   Use the rearranged formula to calculate the number of moles of sodium hydroxide that were added from the burette. The concentration of sodium hydroxide was $1\,mol/dm^3$.

number of moles of sodium hydroxide = ...

....

....

.... [2]

d The chemical equation for the reaction between ethanoic acid and sodium hydroxide is:

$$CH_3COOH(aq) + NaOH(aq) \rightarrow CH_3COONa(aq) + H_2O(l)$$

    i Use the chemical equation for the reaction to calculate how many moles of ethanoic acid react with 1 mole of sodium hydroxide.

    .... **[1]**

    ii State the number of moles of ethanoic acid that reacted with the sodium hydroxide.

    .... **[1]**

e Calculate the concentration of ethanoic acid in the sample.

....

....

.... **[2]**

[Total: 12]

3 A gold ring is for sale. The seller claims that the ring is made from pure gold.

    a The graph shows the temperature of a sample of pure gold as it is gradually heated.

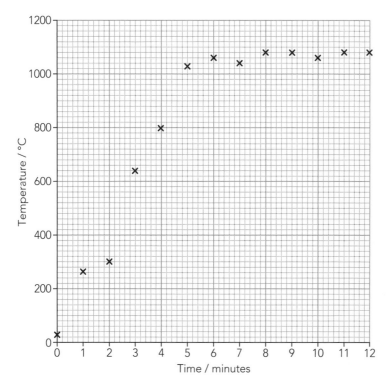

    i Circle any anomalous points. **[1]**

    ii Draw a best-fit line (or curve). **[2]**

    iii Use the graph to determine the approximate melting point of pure gold.

.... [2]

b A buyer wants evidence that the ring is made of pure gold.

    i Explain why finding the melting point is not a suitable method to prove that the ring is made from pure gold.

....

.... [1]

    ii Use the measurements shown to work out if the ring is made of pure gold. The units for the measuring cylinders are in cm³. The density of pure gold is 19.3 g/cm³.

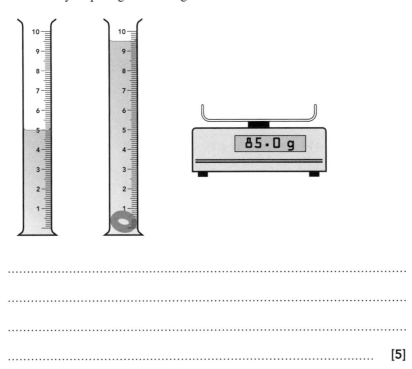

....

....

....

.... [5]

c Pure gold is soft and unsuitable for making jewellery. Gold alloys are used instead.

The composition of an alloy of white gold is shown in the table.

Metal	Percentage
gold	75
palladium	10
nickel	10
zinc	5

i   Sketch the most suitable type of chart to show this data.

[2]

ii   Explain why you chose this type of chart.

....

.... [1]

[Total: 14]

4   The product of a chemical reaction is in the gas state. Two different methods can be used to investigate how rate of reaction changes during the reaction.

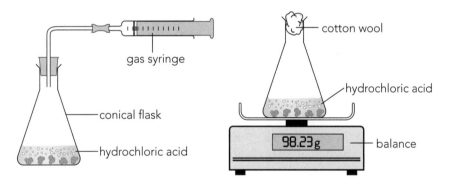

a   Zinc reacts with hydrochloric acid, producing zinc chloride and hydrogen. The balanced chemical equation for the reaction is:

$$Zn(s) + 2HCl(aq) \rightarrow ZnCl_2(aq) + H_2(g)$$

    i   Identify the correct calculation to find the relative formula mass of zinc chloride.

         A $30 + 17 \times 2 = 64$ **B** $65 + 35.5 \times 2 = 136$

         C $(65 + 35.5) \times 2 = 201$ **D** $65 + 35.5 \times 2 = 201$

         .... **[1]**

    ii   The relative molecular mass of hydrogen (H_2) is 2. Give the mass of zinc that produces 2 g of H_2.

         .... **[1]**

    iii Calculate the mass of hydrogen produced by 1 g of zinc.

         ....

         .... **[1]**

b   Calcium carbonate also reacts with hydrochloric acid. The products of the reaction are calcium chloride, carbon dioxide and water. The balanced chemical equation for the reaction is:

$$CaCO_3(s) + 2HCl(aq) \rightarrow CaCl_2(aq) + CO_2(g) + H_2O(l)$$

    i   Show that the relative formula mass of calcium carbonate is 100.

         .... **[1]**

    ii   Calculate the mass of carbon dioxide produced by 100 g of calcium carbonate.

         .... **[1]**

    iii Calculate the mass of carbon dioxide produced by 1 g of calcium carbonate.

         ....

         .... **[1]**

c   Use your answers to parts **a iii** and **b iii** to explain why loss of mass is a suitable method to investigate the rate of reaction of hydrochloric acid with calcium carbonate, but not with zinc.

     ....

     ....

     .... **[2]**

                                                           [Total: 8]

5   Magnesium reacts with hydrochloric acid to make hydrogen. A student performs an experiment to investigate the volume of hydrogen produced each minute. The student used 25 cm³ hydrochloric acid with a concentration of 0.5 mol/dm³. The chemical equation for the reaction is:

$$Mg(s) + 2HCl \rightarrow MgCl_2(aq) + H_2(g)$$

The student's data are shown in the table.

Time / minutes	Volume of hydrogen / cm^3
0	0
1	26
2	64
3	68
4	82
5	86
6	94
7	98
8	100
9	100
10	100

a i   Identify the independent variable.   .... **[1]**

   ii   Identify the dependent variable.   .... **[1]**

   iii Draw axes to show the dependent and independent variables.   **[3]**

   iv   Plot the data points on the graph.   **[1]**

   v   Identify and circle any anomalous results.   **[1]**

   vi   Draw a best-fit curve.

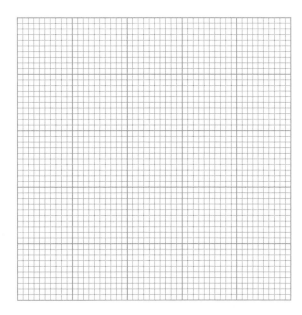

[2]

b **i** Describe how the rate of reaction at 1 minute compares with the rate of reaction at 6 minutes.

....

.... [1]

ii Give the name of the feature of the graph that you compared.

.... [1]

iii Use the graph to determine the time at which the reaction finished.

....

.... [2]

c **i** The student used 0.1 g of magnesium ribbon. Calculate the number of moles of magnesium used.

....

....

.... [2]

ii Use the chemical equation to find the ratio of $Mg:H_2$ .... [1]

iii State the number of moles of hydrogen (H_2) theoretically produced by 0.1 g of magnesium.

.... [1]

d **i** Rearrange the mathematical formula

$$\text{number of moles} = \frac{\text{volume}}{\text{molar volume}} \text{ into the form:}$$

volume = ... [1]

ii Use your answer to part **c iii** to calculate the volume of hydrogen produced in the reaction. The molar volume is $24\,dm^3$.

....

.... [1]

iii Convert your answer to cm^3.

.... [1]

e The student repeated the experiment using acid with a lower concentration ($0.1\,mol/dm^3$).

i Convert the volume of acid used ($25\,cm^3$) to dm^3.

.... [1]

ii   Calculate the number of moles of HCl.

....

....

.... [1]

iii   Give your answer in standard form.   .... [1]

iv   The chemical equation for the reaction is Mg(s) + 2HCl → MgCl$_2$(aq) + H$_2$(g). Calculate number of moles of magnesium needed to react with all the HCl.

....

....

.... [2]

v   Look at your answer to part **c i**. Describe what you would observe when the reaction finished.

....

....

.... [1]

[Total: 26]

6   Ethene is an unsaturated hydrocarbon. When bromine water is added, the bromine water is decolourised.

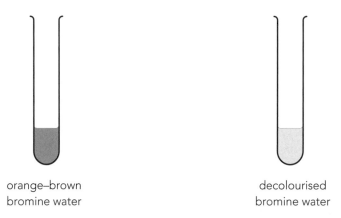

orange–brown
bromine water

decolourised
bromine water

The bromine reacts with the ethene. Bromine does not react with ethane.

a Look at the displayed formulae for ethene, ethane and 1,2-dibromoethane.

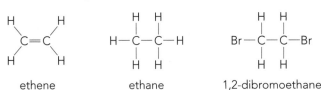

ethene   ethane   1,2-dibromoethane

i Give the chemical formula of each molecule.

ethene .... [1]

ethane .... [1]

1,2-dibromoethane .... [1]

ii Give the ratio of atoms in each molecule.

ethene C : H ...... : ...... [1]

ethane C : H ...... : ...... [1]

1,2-dibromoethane C : H : Br ...... : ...... : ...... [1]

iii Give the empirical formula of each molecule.

ethene .... [1]

ethane .... [1]

1,2-dibromoethane .... [1]

b Look at the reaction pathway diagram for the reaction between ethene and bromine.

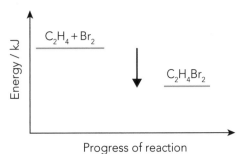

i Use the diagram to determine if the reaction is exothermic or endothermic. .... [1]

ii Describe how you decided if the reaction is exothermic or endothermic.

....

....

....

.... [1]

c

Bond	Bond energy / kJ per mole
Br–Br	193
C–Br	276
C–H	412
C=C	612
C–C	348

Use the bond energy data in the table to calculate:

i   the energy needed to break bonds

....

....

.... **[2]**

ii   the energy given out when bonds form

....

....

.... **[2]**

iii the overall enthalpy change for the reaction.

.... **[1]**

[Total: 16]

7   A student is making copper chloride. The student adds copper carbonate
     to hydrochloric acid until there is excess copper carbonate.

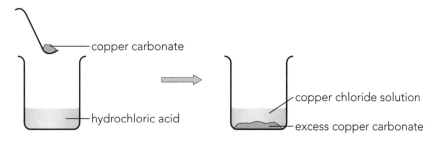

The student then filters the mixture and pours the filtrate into an
evaporating basin.

Finally the student evaporates the water.

The chemical equation for the reaction is:

$$CuCO_3(s) + 2HCl(aq) \rightarrow CuCl_2(aq) + CO_2(g) + H_2O(l)$$

a   The student finds the mass of the evaporating basin, and then finds the total mass of the evaporating basin plus the copper chloride crystals.
Calculate the actual yield of copper chloride.

Mass of evaporating basin	21.30 g
Mass of evaporating basin + copper chloride crystals	27.80 g
Actual yield of copper chloride	

.... **[1]**

b **i**   Use the isotope data to calculate the relative atomic mass of copper.
Record your answer to three significant figures.

Isotope	Abundance / %
copper-63 (^{63}Cu)	69.1
copper-65 (^{65}Cu)	30.9

....

.... **[2]**

    ii   Round your answer to two significant figures. .... **[1]**

c   Calculate the relative formula mass of:

    i   copper carbonate ($CuCO_3$)

.... **[1]**

    ii   copper chloride ($CuCl_2$).

.... **[1]**

d **i**   Calculate the mass of copper chloride formed by 1 g of copper carbonate.

.... **[1]**

    ii   Calculate the theoretical yield of copper chloride formed from 6.2 g of copper carbonate.

....

.... **[1]**

e   Use your answers to parts **a** and **d ii** to calculate the percentage yield
    of copper chloride in this experiment.

    ....

    .... [1]

    [Total: 9]

8   A student adds hydrochloric acid to a polystyrene beaker. The student measures
    the starting temperature, then adds sodium hydroxide solution and stirs the
    mixture. The temperature is measured every minute for 10 minutes.

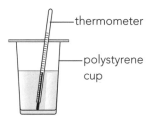

a   i   Read the thermometer scale and record the temperatures in the table.

Time / minutes	Thermometer	Temperature / °C
8	26 — 25	
9	26 — 25	
10	26 — 25	

[3]

ii   Add the three temperatures to the graph.

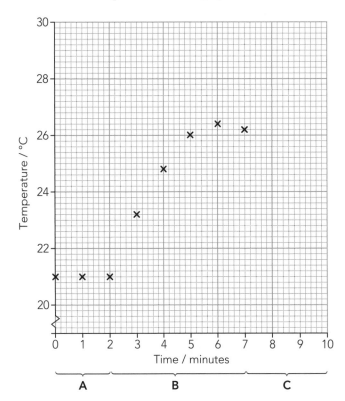

[1]

b   Look at the completed graph. Describe what is shown in each section.

A   .... [1]

B   .... [1]

C   .... [1]

c   i   Draw a best-fit line through the points for 6 minutes to 10 minutes.   [1]

ii   Extrapolate the best-fit line until it reaches the vertical axis.   [1]

iii State the temperature where the line crosses the vertical axis.

.... [1]

iv   This temperature is the maximum temperature. Explain why the maximum temperature was not actually reached.

....

.... [1]

[Total: 11]

9   Aspirin (acetylsalicylic acid) is a commonly used drug for the treatment of pain
    and fever. An aspirin tablet is dissolved using an ethanol solvent. It is then diluted
    with distilled water to make a volume of $25.0\,cm^3$ in a conical flask. The tablet is
    titrated against $0.1\,mol/dm^3$ sodium hydroxide solution from a burette.

   a   i   Draw a table to record three titration measurements and a mean.

                                                                                    [2]

      ii   Read the measurements from the burettes shown and add the data
           to the table.

           Titration 1   Titration 2   Titration 3

             ─ 16   ─ 16   ─ 16

             ─ 17   ─ 17   ─ 17   [3]

      iii   Calculate the mean titration volume and add the data to the table.   [1]

   b   i   Calculate the number of moles of sodium hydroxide titrated.

           ....

           ....   [2]

      ii   Aspirin reacts with sodium hydroxide in a $1:1$ ratio. State the number
           of moles of aspirin in the conical flask.

           ....   [1]

      iii   Calculate the concentration of the aspirin solution in the flask.

           ....

           ....

           ....   [1]

c   i   The chemical formula of aspirin is $C_9H_8O_4$. Calculate the relative formula mass of aspirin.

.... [1]

ii Use the number of moles of aspirin to calculate the actual mass of aspirin that was dissolved.

....

....

.... [1]

iii The aspirin tablet that dissolved had a mass of 310 mg. Write this mass in grams (g).   .... [1]

iv Calculate the percentage purity of the aspirin tablet.

....

....

.... [1]

[Total: 14]

10 Blue copper sulfate crystals have the formula $CuSO_4 \cdot 5H_2O$. The crystals contain water molecules.

a   i   State the ratio of $CuSO_4$ to H_2O.   .... : .... [1]

ii State the number of moles of H_2O in 1 mole of $CuSO_4 \cdot 5H_2O$.

.... [1]

iii Calculate the relative formula mass of $CuSO_4 \cdot 5H_2O$.

....

.... [1]

iv Calculate the number of moles of $CuSO_4 \cdot 5H_2O$ in 1 g of blue copper sulfate crystals.

....

.... [1]

v   Use Avogadro's constant (6.02×10^{23}) to calculate the number of H_2O molecules in 1 g of blue copper sulfate crystals.

....

.... [1]

b   After carefully heating the crystals, the blue copper sulfate crystals turn white.
    White copper sulfate contains no water molecules.

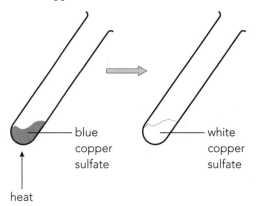

blue copper sulfate

white copper sulfate

heat

Calculate the percentage by mass of copper in:

i   blue copper sulfate ($CuSO_4 \cdot 5H_2O$)

....

.... [1]

ii white copper sulfate ($CuSO_4$).

....

....

.... [2]

[Total: 8]

> Glossary

Command words

Below are the Cambridge International definitions for command words which may be used in exams. The information in this section is taken from the Cambridge International syllabus (0620/0971) for examination from 2023. You should always refer to the appropriate syllabus document for the year of your examination to confirm the details and for more information. The syllabus document is available on the Cambridge International website www.cambridgeinternational.org.

analyse: examine in detail to show meaning, identify elements and the relationship between them

calculate: work out from given facts, figures or information

compare: identify/comment on similarities and/or differences

consider: review and respond to given information

contrast: identify/comment on differences

deduce: conclude from available information

define: give precise meaning

demonstrate: show how or give an example

describe: state the points of a topic / give characteristics and main features

determine: establish an answer using the information available

evaluate: judge or calculate the quality, importance, amount, or value of something

examine: investigate closely, in detail

explain: set out purposes or reasons / make the relationships between things evident / provide why and/or how and support with relevant evidence

give: produce an answer from a given source or recall/memory

identify: name / select / recognise

justify: support a case with evidence/argument

predict: suggest what may happen based on available information

show (that): provide structured evidence that leads to a given result

sketch: make a simple freehand drawing showing the key features, taking care over proportions

state: express in clear terms

suggest: apply knowledge and understanding to situations where there are a range of valid responses in order to make proposals / put forward considerations

Key Words

accuracy: how close a value is to the true value

angle: a measure of the amount of turn between two adjoining or intersecting lines; this may be determined, in degrees, using a protractor

anomalous result: (1) one of a series of repeated experimental experimental results that is much larger or smaller than the others (2) a point on a graph that is considered unusual compared with the trend of other values

area: a measure of the size of a surface (measured in square units, e.g. cm^2 or m^2)

axis: a reference line on a graph or chart, along which a distance scale represents values of a variable

bar chart: a chart with separated rectangular bars of equal width; the height (or length) of a bar represents the value of the variable

best-fit line: a straight line or a smooth curve drawn on a graph that passes through or close to as many of the data points as possible; it represents the best estimate of the relationship between the variables

BIDMAS: 'Brackets, Indices, Division/Multiplication, Addition/Subtraction', which is the order in which mathematical operations are done in a multi-step calculation

categorical data: data that can be grouped into categories (types) but not ordered

circumference: the distance around a circle

continuous data: data that can take any numerical value within a range

controlled variable: a variable that is kept constant in an investigation

coordinates: values that determine the position of a data point on a graph, relative to the axes

decimal: a number expressed using a system of counting based on the number 10 where the number of tenths, hundredths, thousandths, etc., are represented as digits following a decimal point; the digits after the decimal point are also known as a decimal fraction

decimal place: the place-value position of a number after a decimal point; the number 6.357 has three decimal places

decimal point: a symbol (dot) used in a decimal number that separates a whole number and its fractional part

dependent variable: the variable that is measured or observed in an investigation, when the independent variable is changed

derived unit: a new unit created by multiplying or dividing two or more SI base units

diameter: a straight line connecting two points on a circle (or sphere) that passes through the centre

digit: any of the numerals from 0 to 9 used to make a number

directly proportional: the relationship between two variables such that when one doubles, the other doubles; the graph of the two variables is a straight line through the origin

discrete data: data that can take only certain values

equation: a mathematical statement, using an '=' sign, showing that two expressions are equal; an equation that shows the relationship between variables

estimate: (find) an approximate value

extrapolate: extending the line of best fit on a graph beyond the range of the data, in order to estimate values not within the data set

formula (mathematical): an equation that shows the relationship between real-world variables. For example, concentration = (number of moles/volume) is a mathematical formula

gradient: the slope (steepness) of a line on a graph; it is calculated by dividing the vertical change by the horizontal change

horizontal axis: the line that is arranged from left to right on a graph. This is also known as the x-axis

hypotenuse: the longest side of a triangle that has one angle of 90°; the side opposite the right angle in a right-angled triangle

independent variable: the variable in an investigation that is changed by the experimenter

index: a small raised number that indicates the power, for example, the index 4 here shows that the 2 is raised to the power 4, which means four 2s multiplied together: $2^4 = 2 \times 2 \times 2 \times 2$

intercept: the point at which a line on a graph crosses one of the axes; usually refers to the intercept with the vertical (y-) axis

interpolate: on a graph, to estimate the value of a variable from the value of the other variable, using a best-fit line; on a scale, to estimate a measurement that falls between two scale marks

intersect: where two lines on a graph meet or cross one another

inversely proportional: the relationship between two variables such that when one doubles, the other halves

line graph: a graph of one variable against another where the data points fall on or close to a single line, which may be straight, curved or straight-line segments between points, depending on the relationship between the variables

linear relationship: a relationship between two variables that can be represented on a graph by a straight line

mean: an average value: the sum of a set of values divided by the number of values in the set

meniscus: the curved surface of a liquid, for example in a tube or cylinder

non-linear relationship: a relationship between two variables that can be represented on a graph by a curved line; two quantities are not proportional to each other in a non-linear relationship

operation: a mathematical process, such as addition or multiplication, in which one set of numbers is produced from another

origin: the point on a graph at which the value of both variables is zero and where the axes cross

percentage: a fraction expressed out of 100, e.g. $\frac{1}{2} = \frac{50}{100} = 50\%$

pie chart: a circular chart that is divided into sectors which represent the relative values of components: the angle of the sector is proportional to the value of the component

place value: the value of a digit depending on its position within a number, for example, in 476, there are 4 hundreds, 7 tens and 6 units

power: a number raised to the power 2 is squared (e.g. x^2); a number raised to the power 3 is cubed (e.g. x^3); and so on

power of ten: a number such as 10^3 or 10^{-3}

precision: the closeness of agreement between several measured values obtained by repeated measurements; the precision of a single value can be indicated by the number of significant figures given in the number, for example 4.027 has greater precision (is more precise) than 4.0

processed data: data produced by calculation using raw experimental data

qualitative data: data that are descriptive and not numerical

quantitative data: data that are numerical

radius: the distance from the centre of a circle (or sphere) to the circle (or sphere surface)

random error: measurement error that varies in an unpredictable way from one measurement to the next

range: the interval between the lowest value and the highest value, for example, of a measured variable or on the scale of a measuring instrument

rate: a measure of how much one variable changes relative to another variable; usually how quickly a variable changes as time progresses

ratio: a comparison of two numbers or of two measurements with the same unit; the ratio of A to B can be written $A:B$ or expressed as a fraction $\frac{A}{B}$

raw data: data collected by measurement or observation

rearrange: to manipulate an equation mathematically so that the unknown value can be calculated; also termed 'change the subject'

reciprocal: 1 divided by a value; for example, the reciprocal of A is $\frac{1}{A}$

right angle: at 90° to (or perpendicular)

rounding: expressing a number as an approximation, with fewer significant figures; for example, 7.436 rounded to two significant figures is 7.4, or rounded to three significant figures is 7.44

sector: section of a pie chart ('pie slice'); the different sectors make up the total value of the whole pie chart

scale: a set of marks with equal intervals, for example, on a graph axis or a measuring cylinder, or, on a scale diagram, the ratio of a length in the diagram to the actual size

scientific notation: another term for standard form

significant figures (sf): the number of digits in a number, not including any zeros at the beginning; for example, the number of significant figures in 0.0682 is three

standard form: notation in which a number is written as a number between 1 and 10 multiplied by a power of ten; for example, 4.78×10^9; also called scientific notation, or standard index form, or standard notation

standard index form: another term for standard form

surface area: the total area of the surface of a three-dimensional object

systematic error: measurement error that results in measured values differing from the true value by the same amount each time a measurement is made; this may occur for example when a balance reads 0.02 g with no mass on it

tangent line: a straight line that touches the curve on a graph at only one point and that has the same gradient (slope) as the gradient of the curve at that point

trend: a pattern shown by data; on a graph this may be shown by points following a 'trend line', the best estimate of this being the best-fit line

uncertainty: range of variation in experimental results because of sources of error; the true value is expected to be within this range

unit: a standard used in measuring a variable, for example, the metre or the volt

unit prefix: a prefix (term added to the front of a word) added to a unit name to indicate a power of ten of that unit, e.g. 1 millimetre = 10^{-3} metre

variable: the word used for any measurable quantity; its value can vary or change

vertical axis: the line that is arranged from top to bottom on a graph. This is also known as the y-axis

volume: a measure of three-dimensional space (measured in cubic units, e.g. cm^3 or m^3)

x-axis: the line that is arranged from left to right on a graph; also known as the horizontal axis

y-axis: the line that is arranged from top to bottom on a graph; also known as the vertical axis

The Periodic Table of Elements

Key

atomic number
atomic symbol
name
relative atomic mass

I	II	III	IV	V	VI	VII	VIII
							2 **He** helium 4
3 **Li** lithium 7	4 **Be** beryllium 9	5 **B** boron 11	6 **C** carbon 12	7 **N** nitrogen 14	8 **O** oxygen 16	9 **F** fluorine 19	10 **Ne** neon 20
11 **Na** sodium 23	12 **Mg** magnesium 24	13 **Al** aluminium 27	14 **Si** silicon 28	15 **P** phosphorus 31	16 **S** sulfur 32	17 **Cl** chlorine 35.5	18 **Ar** argon 40

1 **H** hydrogen 1

Transition elements (Period 4–7):

	I	II											III	IV	V	VI	VII	VIII

Period 4: 19 **K** potassium 39 · 20 **Ca** calcium 40 · 21 **Sc** scandium 45 · 22 **Ti** titanium 48 · 23 **V** vanadium 51 · 24 **Cr** chromium 52 · 25 **Mn** manganese 55 · 26 **Fe** iron 56 · 27 **Co** cobalt 59 · 28 **Ni** nickel 59 · 29 **Cu** copper 64 · 30 **Zn** zinc 65 · 31 **Ga** gallium 70 · 32 **Ge** germanium 73 · 33 **As** arsenic 75 · 34 **Se** selenium 79 · 35 **Br** bromine 80 · 36 **Kr** krypton 84

Period 5: 37 **Rb** rubidium 85 · 38 **Sr** strontium 88 · 39 **Y** yttrium 89 · 40 **Zr** zirconium 91 · 41 **Nb** niobium 93 · 42 **Mo** molybdenum 96 · 43 **Tc** technetium – · 44 **Ru** ruthenium 101 · 45 **Rh** rhodium 103 · 46 **Pd** palladium 106 · 47 **Ag** silver 108 · 48 **Cd** cadmium 112 · 49 **In** indium 115 · 50 **Sn** tin 119 · 51 **Sb** antimony 122 · 52 **Te** tellurium 128 · 53 **I** iodine 127 · 54 **Xe** xenon 131

Period 6: 55 **Cs** caesium 133 · 56 **Ba** barium 137 · 57–71 lanthanoids · 72 **Hf** hafnium 178 · 73 **Ta** tantalum 181 · 74 **W** tungsten 184 · 75 **Re** rhenium 186 · 76 **Os** osmium 190 · 77 **Ir** iridium 192 · 78 **Pt** platinum 195 · 79 **Au** gold 197 · 80 **Hg** mercury 201 · 81 **Tl** thallium 204 · 82 **Pb** lead 207 · 83 **Bi** bismuth 209 · 84 **Po** polonium – · 85 **At** astatine – · 86 **Rn** radon –

Period 7: 87 **Fr** francium – · 88 **Ra** radium – · 89–103 actinoids · 104 **Rf** rutherfordium – · 105 **Db** dubnium – · 106 **Sg** seaborgium – · 107 **Bh** bohrium – · 108 **Hs** hassium – · 109 **Mt** meitnerium – · 110 **Ds** darmstadtium – · 111 **Rg** roentgenium – · 112 **Cn** copernicium – · 113 **Nh** nihonium – · 114 **Fl** flerovium – · 115 **Mc** moscovium – · 116 **Lv** livermorium – · 117 **Ts** tennessine – · 118 **Og** oganesson –

lanthanoids: 57 **La** lanthanum 139 · 58 **Ce** cerium 140 · 59 **Pr** praseodymium 141 · 60 **Nd** neodymium 144 · 61 **Pm** promethium – · 62 **Sm** samarium 150 · 63 **Eu** europium 152 · 64 **Gd** gadolinium 157 · 65 **Tb** terbium 159 · 66 **Dy** dysprosium 163 · 67 **Ho** holmium 165 · 68 **Er** erbium 167 · 69 **Tm** thulium 169 · 70 **Yb** ytterbium 173 · 71 **Lu** lutetium 175

actinoids: 89 **Ac** actinium – · 90 **Th** thorium 232 · 91 **Pa** protactinium 231 · 92 **U** uranium 238 · 93 **Np** neptunium – · 94 **Pu** plutonium – · 95 **Am** americium – · 96 **Cm** curium – · 97 **Bk** berkelium – · 98 **Cf** californium – · 99 **Es** einsteinium – · 100 **Fm** fermium – · 101 **Md** mendelevium – · 102 **No** nobelium – · 103 **Lr** lawrencium –

The volume of one mole of any gas is $24\,dm^3$ at room temperature and pressure (r.t.p.).

> Acknowledgements

The authors and publishers acknowledge the following sources of copyright material and are grateful for the permissions granted. While every effort has been made, it has not always been possible to identify the sources of all the material used, or to trace all copyright holders. If any omissions are brought to our notice, we will be happy to include the appropriate acknowledgements on reprinting.

Thanks to the following for permission to reproduce images:

Cover Photo: Laguna Design/Getty Images

Martyn F. Chillmaid / Science photo library; Sputnik / Science photo library.